SCIENCE IN YOUR OWN BACK YARD

Also by Elizabeth K. Cooper

MINERALS
(with Herbert S. Zim)

SCIENCE IN
YOUR OWN BACK YARD

BY ELIZABETH K. COOPER

with illustrations by the author

NEW YORK HB HARCOURT, BRACE AND COMPANY

To Bess and Pat

*and the wonderful things we
discovered in our own back yards*

First edition

LIBRARY OF CONGRESS CATALOG CARD NUMBER: 58-5705
PRINTED IN THE UNITED STATES OF AMERICA BY THE MURRAY PRINTING COMPANY

CONTENTS

FOREWORD

By exploring the part of the world that is in your yard and in your neighborhood, you can discover something about every subject in the right-hand column below.

The Scientist	The Science	The Subject Studied
Astronomer	Astronomy	Stars and other heavenly bodies
Botanist	Botany	Plant Life
Entomologist	Entomology	Insect life
Geologist	Geology	Rocks and earth structures
Herpetologist	Herpetology	Snakes and other reptiles
Meteorologist	Meteorology	Weather and other atmospheric conditions
Mineralogist	Mineralogy	Minerals found in the earth's crust
Ornithologist	Ornithology	Bird life
Paleontologist	Paleontology	Fossils
Zoologist	Zoology	Animal life

Some of these subjects may interest you more than others. If so, you will want to do extra exploring in your field of special interest. There are books that will help you and special subjects you can study in school. There are also many experiments that will lead you to discover things by yourself. From astronomer to zoologist, which would you like to be? The experiments and explorations in this book may help you to decide.

1

EXPLORING THE YARD ON YOUR STOMACH

Nearly everybody has a back yard. If you haven't, you probably know where there is a vacant lot. Or you may go to a park or to a school playground. Wherever you go outdoors, that's the place to begin your exploring.

An explorer looks very carefully at everything around him. Sometimes he is prospecting for treasures like gold or diamonds or uranium. You will be surprised at how many treasures of a different sort you can find in your own back yard. You will discover scientific wonders right under your feet and over your head that are a great deal more important than gems and precious metals. You will find clues to the scientific laws that make it possible for you and me and all living things to exist on this planet we call Earth. And you will be learning to work as a scientist works.

A good explorer uses scientific methods. He learns all he can about the things he is studying. He takes notes and keeps records. He talks with other scientists. He uses tools. He experiments to find answers to his questions. In all he does, he learns how to make careful observations.

How can you observe the world around you here in your

small back yard? How can you discover everything that *is* around you so that you can choose what interests you most?

First of all, stretch out flat on your stomach right in the middle of your yard. You can make your first scientific observations by using your own five senses.

What do you see?

What do you hear?

What do you feel?

What do you smell?

What do you taste?

One boy saw these things as he lay on his stomach:

Different kinds of grass

Spots of bare earth between the grass

A ladybug beetle

An ant climbing a blade of grass

Some white stones

A very small fly

A dead bee

A clump of ferns

Drops of water from the sprinkler

A toadstool

A white-headed dandelion

A tiny lizard

Then his dog came over and licked his ear and tickled him so that he sat up suddenly. So, of course, he had also seen a dog, medium size!

A girl who listened carefully said that she heard these sounds:

Water dripping from leaves
Wind blowing through the trees
Insects buzzing
A baby crying
People talking
Some birds chirping
A puppy barking
Most young explorers who begin with looking and lis-

tening get long lists of things they see and hear as they lie on the grass. Our eyes and ears are our most useful sense organs for collecting information. Touch, smell, and taste give us fewer impressions. But you can get clues from these senses, too.

Can you feel these things?

    The smoothness of a stone

    The rough bark of a tree

    The soft fur of a cat

    The cool wetness of mud

    The stinging sharpness of a thistle

If you were a dog or one of the many other kinds of animals with keen noses, you would be able to learn as much by your sense of smell as you do now by seeing and hearing. Since you are a member of the human family, your nose is not nearly as sensitive as your eyes and ears. But if you close your eyes and concentrate on smells, perhaps you can train yourself to pick up clues by careful smelling.

Can your nose tell you the difference between these things?

    Dry earth

    Damp grass

    Clay

    Chrysanthemum leaves

    Your dog

    Roses, pansies, and other flowers

Of course, if you should happen to be near a hard-shelled black beetle called a stink-bug, your nose would get a clue — a strong one — without any trouble at all. (And you would know at once how the insect got its name.) But most of the things that live and grow in your yard will not have a strong smell like the stink-bug's. There will be many soft, delicate smells, and you can learn to tell them apart.

As for the sense of taste, you might put your tongue on a stone you picked up at the seashore and get a faint taste of salt. Or you might wash some nasturtium leaves, clover leaves, and blades of grass and taste tiny bits of them. Some are spicy and some are sour. Some flower petals have a special taste. But it is not a good idea to go around tasting strange plants, leaves, flowers, or insects. Ants are supposed to have a sour taste, but you certainly wouldn't want to taste one. You had better not try to use your sense of taste in your back-yard exploring. You might just happen to bite into something that is deadly poison, like an oleander bush or a member of the toad-stool family. They are not marked with a skull and cross-bones as poisons are marked in the kitchen or in the family medicine chest. By the time you found out something you'd tasted was poisonous, it would be too late and you'd be in serious trouble. So remember, you have a good sense of taste, but you also have *good sense* in general, and so you will do your tasting on things that you know are good to eat.

Go back to *seeing* now, as you lie on your stomach. What does the grass look like when you examine it close-ly? Can you see the separate little plants? Do you see where the roots go down into the soil and where the plant spreads out and the little blades grow upward toward the sun? Have the blades been cut short by the lawn mower? Are there any spots you can see where the grass has been allowed to grow, perhaps at the foot of a tree or along a fence or flower bed? What does this uncut grass look like? Does it have stems and tiny flowers? Can you see any seeds?

Look down into the grass right under your nose. Are there any tiny plants growing on the ground between the grass plants? Watch for an ant in the grass. How does it travel? If you were as small as the ant, the grass would seem like a jungle. See how the ant scampers in and out among the tiny plants. Sometimes it climbs clear to the top of a blade of grass, over the top, and down the other side. What a dense, overgrown trail the little ant has to travel!

Do you have any clover with its three-lobed leaves and tiny white flowers there in your grass? Pick one of the little flowers and smell its sweetness. If you find a leaf with four lobes, a four-leafed clover, it is supposed to bring you good luck. How many different kinds of tiny plants can you find growing there in your lawn? How do you think they got there?

Look for some more ants. Are they all the same size, kind, and color? What differences can you find among them? Can you hear a faint buzzing of other insects? Perhaps some flying insects are darting in and out — flies, gnats, ladybugs, butterflies, bees. You may have the

good fortune to catch sight of a quick little lizard going after a fly for his lunch, or a garden snail leaving a silvery path behind him as he moves slowly from plant to plant. If your eyes and ears are sharp, you will discover a busy world of life and motion there beneath you in the grass.

Sometimes scientists use powerful magnifying lenses to study this lively world among the slender blades of

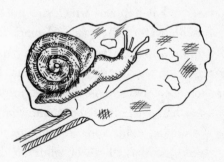

grass. You can look at the grass through a hand magnifying lens. There may be one in your house. If not, you can buy one in a ten-cent store or in a stationery store. Then sprinkle a few grains of sugar around and see what happens. Some ants may carry the bits of sugar to their homes underground. Other insects may come to sip the sweetness as soon as the moisture in the grass melts the sugar grains. If you decide that you want to do your exploring in the insect world, there are many other experiments that you can make. But first, see what other wonders there are to explore as you lie on your stomach.

Do you know where you are? Where in the world? Where in the universe? You are a tiny, tiny speck on the outer surface of a huge moving ball. You are stretched out on the crust of the earth. What is the crust of the earth? Look at it, under the grass. What do you see? You know, of course, that the roots of grass and other plants grow in dirt, or soil as it is properly called. Do you know what soil is made of? Put some in your hand. Feel it with your fingers. Look at it through your magnifying glass. Do you see different kinds of particles or bits of material? What happens when you put some soil in a glass jar with water? How is soil made? Can you make soil? You can answer these and many more questions by doing some interesting experiments. They are worth doing, too, because soil is the most important resource in the earth's crust. It is more important to man than all the diamonds, gold, and uranium in the world.

Important though soil is, there is relatively little of it

on the earth. The merest film of soil clings to the earth's crust. And not all of the crust either, for there are miles and miles of granite mountain peaks with no soil on them at all. But here in your yard you can see the soil, and if you have ever dug a hole in the ground, you know that more soil lies under the surface. If you dig deep enough, however, you will hit solid rock, for rock is under the soil, here in your yard and all over the world. A study of the earth's crust, then, includes a study of rock.

There are different kinds of rocks, formed in different ways. If you decide to collect and study rocks, you will find out about these differences. If you stretch out your hands, perhaps you can pick up a few pebbles or stones. Even though they are small, they are all rocks to the scientist. Look at them carefully. If they are covered with dirt, wash them until you can see what they really look like. If you have quite a few rocks from different places, you will notice that rocks differ from each other in color, in the way they feel, and in weight. Yet they have all come from the earth's crust. There are interesting reasons why there are so many differences among your rocks. And there are some interesting ways in which you can find out what these reasons are.

2

EXPLORING THE YARD
ON YOUR BACK

When you are tired of lying on your stomach, roll over on your back. What do you see and hear and smell now? Perhaps you are near a tree and can look up into its leafy branches. What do the leaves look like? Do you know that no two of them are exactly alike? Are they still or are they moving in the wind? Do they make a sound as they move? What else do you see in the tree — buds, flowers, fruit, cones, seeds? It will depend, of course, not only on how sharp your eyes are, but on the kind of tree and the time of year. Notice how the trunk grows, how the limbs branch out from the trunk and the smaller limbs and twigs grow out from the main limbs. Every kind of tree has its own pattern and its own beauty.

Perhaps you can catch a glimpse of a bird winging across the sky or diving into the leafy greenness of the tree. As you gaze upward, you may find an old nest hanging loosely from the branches or from the eaves of your house. Have you ever examined a bird's nest closely? If you took one apart very carefully, you could find out what it is made of and the number of separate trips the bird had to make to collect the material. If you do take one apart, do you think you can put it back together again so that it looks like a nest once more? Well, have you ever *tried?*

Do you ever wonder what kinds of birds live in your neighborhood? Have you ever fed them and given them a place to drink and bathe? Have you ever watched the birds coming and going, flying, landing, eating, feeding their babies? There are scientists who spend their lives studying birds. Yet even to such scientists there are still many bird mysteries waiting to be solved. Perhaps it's the mystery of birds, as well as their color and beauty of flight, that makes them interesting to so many people. There are thousands of men and women all over who are

19

not bird scientists but bird watchers. They watch birds by the hour through field glasses or opera glasses, or they use cameras. They learn a great deal about bird life through these activities. They are proud to be called bird watchers. Maybe you would like to be one, too.

What else do you see as you lie there on your back? Look toward a fence or some bushes. You may find a delicate spider web stretched like fairy lace. Perhaps the spider that spun it is right there in the web, a rather ugly

and dangerous-looking creature to have woven such a beautiful net. If you watch carefully, you may see a fly or other insect get caught in the web. That will be a dinner for the spider. You can watch a single spider and her web for days and days and keep track of the insects that become entangled in the fine, sticky net. There are many interesting things to be learned about spiders. But they are not creatures to be held in your hands, for one kind has a poisonous bite, and others can give you red, itchy, burning bumps if they bite you. But they are worth watching, especially with your magnifying glass.

Now let your head drop back into the grass and look straight up into the sky. Are there any clouds? What kind are they? Are they soft and puffy like wads of cotton? Or slim strands, layer on layer? Or some other kind? Do you know that cloud formations have names? Do you know what makes clouds? You can find out if you wish.

There is so much to explore in the sky. If you can come back to this same spot after it gets dark, you will find a wonderland of sky and stars and perhaps moonlight. It's all yours to enjoy and study and explore. There are even star maps for you to follow from one group of stars to another as your mind travels with your eyes across the sky at night.

But now it is still daylight and you are still doing your first exploring in your own back yard. You have things in your yard that aren't mentioned here. You will have to find them for yourself. Nearly everything you see or hear or smell or feel or taste can lead you to some science adventure. Take plenty of time to explore, to find out what you have around you. Soon you will be ready to set up your outdoor laboratory. Then you will have a place to work as you collect materials and begin your experiments.

3

SUGGESTIONS FOR A BACK-YARD LABORATORY

Most of the outdoor experimenting suggested in this book can be done anywhere in your yard. You do not need a laboratory in order to explore, but making and using one is fun. It is also convenient to have a regular place to work, with the materials you need close at hand.

The place you choose will depend on the kind of weather you have. While you can work almost anywhere, you must be sure that wind and rain cannot harm your materials, so you will want to be close to shelter of some sort. If your climate is hot, you may want to work under a shade tree. If you have pleasant weather for many days at a time, almost any place in the yard will be comfortable. Here are some possible locations to consider:

Back of the house or back of the garage, against a wall

On the back or side porch of your house

In a tent in the yard

On a terrace or patio

Beside a shed, tool house, barn, or garage, where you can quickly move inside in case of bad weather

You will, of course, want to consult your parents about the place you choose. They may have some suggestions to make. If you plan to work with other boys or girls in the neighborhood, it may be a good idea to get together first and discuss the best place for your work area.

It will be a help to you if your laboratory is near an outdoor faucet or hose. You will need fresh water for many of your experiments. A hose with water running into a bucket on the lawn makes a good "sink" for washing things. The overflow can water the lawn. If there is danger of puddles forming, dig some kind of small drainage trench to carry away the overflow.

Once you have decided on a convenient location, you are ready to plan a work bench or table and a place to sit down while you are working. Materials for these can be found in a number of places if you know where to look. There are attics, basements, garages, and storage sheds — or your local grocery — where you may find wooden boxes and old furniture to use. Consider such things as the following:

> An old kitchen table
> A discarded ironing board, placed on top of two orange crates
> A large sawhorse, with a wide board nailed to the top
> Three orange crates, standing upright, nailed together, and with a board across the top

You may want to stand up while you work. Otherwise, use wooden boxes or old stools or chairs for seats.

You will need some shelves for storing tools and equipment and for displaying your collections. Orange crates may be used. Lay the crates on their sides and stack them, one on top of another. Three orange crates, stacked up and nailed together, make a strong storage place, with six separate compartments. Of course, you may find some old bookcases or book shelves that you'll be allowed to use. If you are this lucky, you will not have to do much building.

All you really need for a good laboratory is a smooth, table-like area to work on and some shelf space. Then you can collect the equipment you need and you are ready to go ahead.

The one piece of scientific equipment you *must* have is a hand-lens magnifying glass. This is essential for your explorations. A good hand lens will make things look large and clear. You will use it as an adult scientist uses his microscope. A good hand lens can be bought at a stationery store for $2.00 to $3.00. You will want one that is two and a half to three inches in diameter and "normal" or "extra powerful" in magnifying strength. It will

be marked on the box. Cheaper, smaller, and less powerful hand lenses can be bought in the dime store. Get a
large, good one if you can. If not, use the best one that
you can afford. Even a small lens will help you to discover many things.

Other tools and equipment are listed below. You will
not need all of them at any one time. But it is well to
gather together at least some of the things you will use
and keep them in order in boxes on your shelves.

Old spoons
Scissors (blunt-pointed)
Paper clips
Garden trowel
Single-edge razor blades
Stapler (useful but not essential)
Kitchen knife
Sieve or flour sifter
Ordinary hammer or geologist's hammer
Tacks and nails
Wire
String
Scotch tape
Pencils and pen
Notebook
Glue or transparent cement
Crayons
Water-color paints and brushes

Since you will be collecting many different kinds of
soil, rocks, seeds, flowers, plants, insects, etc., you will

need all kinds of boxes, trays, bottles, cages, and jars. Most of these containers can be found among the things your family would normally throw away. Get the habit of collecting and saving all the clean containers you can find at home. Your neighborhood stores may be able to give you some, and you can ask your friends and relatives to save them for you. You will be surprised at the number of useful things that are thrown away every day. Here are some of the kinds of containers you will want to save:

Aluminum-foil pans and trays (from TV dinners, frozen desserts, chicken pies, etc.)

Tin pie plates

Flowerpots, any size

Plastic cans and jars (from frozen desserts, ready-made salads, sour cream, etc.)

Peanut butter and mayonnaise jars with lids

Mason canning jars—pint, quart, and half-gallon sizes

Pill bottles, glass or plastic, with corks or lids

Metal cans from Band-Aids

Coffee cans with lids

Tin cans, clean, and with tops smoothly removed

Old china plates or saucers

Old cooking pots or pans

Egg cartons

Wooden cigar boxes

Cardboard boxes from all kinds of products

There are many odds and ends that will be useful to have around. It helps to have ready a box of miscellaneous materials like the following:

Newspapers and magazines

Corrugated cardboard from cartons

Sheets of plain cardboard, cut from large boxes

Cellophane

Drawing paper, poster paper, tag board, colored construction paper

Gummed labels

Wax paper and small cellophane bags

Pieces of wire screen or plastic screen

But the most important and most valuable "scientific tools" you use in exploring cannot be collected or bought. They are an ability to see, hear, smell, taste, and feel, and a well-developed curiosity about the many wonderful things around you.

4

SOIL AND ROCK

Rocks and rock materials form the entire crust of the earth. You walk on it, dig into it, climb on it. People build houses on it, put mines down into it, and cut tunnels through it. Man and all the other animals of the world live on it or in it. It is truly our Mother Earth. And our Mother Earth is rock.

There are many places on the earth's crust where you can see the bare, hard, solid rock, especially in great granite mountain peaks. There are other places where the earth's crust is low and has been filled with vast bodies of water, the oceans of the world. Still other places have streams and rivers that have cut down through the crust, showing different layers of rock.

But here in your yard, the part of the earth's crust you see is a layer of soil. Most men live only where there is soil, for it is there that plants can grow. All people and animals depend upon other animals and plants for food, clothing, and shelter. Soil, or this ordinary "dirt" as you may call it, is really the most important part of the earth's crust. Without soil we could not live on this planet.

Try this experiment to find out what soil is made of. In a tin pie plate, or in the lid of a peanut-butter jar, spread a few spoonfuls of soil from your yard. Crumble it with your fingers. Look at it carefully through your magnifying glass. Do you see different kinds of material in your soil sample? Check the kinds of material you find — pebbles or bits of rock; sand; clay; pieces of roots, leaves, or other parts of plants; insects or parts of insects; or anything else.

Here is another experiment to find out about the different kinds of soil.

Get samples of soil from different places in your yard and from different places in your neighborhood. Try to find a sample that is yellow or tan, one that is dark brown, one that is almost black. Examine each sample and find as many differences as you can. Add a little water to each. Do some get sticky? Do some seem sandy? Do some use up the water more quickly than others?

Leave your soil sample in the sun for several days until the water has evaporated. You will find that some of your samples dry out more quickly than others.

You can make a collection by putting samples of different kinds of soil into small plastic or glass jars. Examine each sample first and find out whether it is:

Clay Soil — very fine and light in color; gets quite sticky when made into mud

Gravel Soil — coarse, with pebbles in it

Sandy Soil — feels gritty; you can see the grains of sand with your magnifying glass

Loam Soil — a mixture of sand and clay

Humus Soil — dark and loose; made from bits of decayed plant and animal material

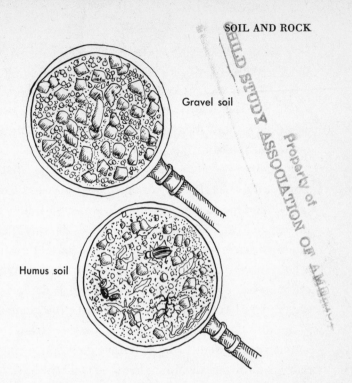

Gravel soil

Humus soil

These are the common garden soils. If you take trips to the desert, mountains, or seashore, or any interesting places away from home, you may want to collect other samples of soil and sand. If you try, you can find earth samples of many different shades of red, brown, and yellow, which are often called "earth colors."

Our next experiment is to show how sand, gravel, and clay are made.

Take two pieces of common sandstone. Rub them together above a piece of plain paper. After you have rubbed hard for a while, what do you find on the paper? Feel it with your fingers. Look at it through your glass.

31

It is sand. Thus pieces of sandstone, rubbed together by the waves of the sea, or knocked together over and over again in a stream, or rolled together down a slope, make sand. Put some soft chunks of sandstone in a can and shake them hard many times. You will find sand on the bottom of the can.

Put some crumbly rocks on top of a large, flat rock. Cover with several layers of newspaper or a piece of burlap. Pound the soft rocks with a hammer until they are as fine as you can make them. Then brush the tiny pieces of fine rock material into a flowerpot or a small tin can with a hole in the bottom. Water this mixture and plant some radish seeds or dried beans in it. Keep it damp but not soggy. You have made soil, and it will grow plants. This is the way the main part of soil is made — from rock.

But if you want to have really good soil — the kind that grows strong, healthy plants — you will have to add vegetable material or animal material or both. That is why gardeners use peat moss, steer manure, bonemeal, and other substances to mix with sandy or clay soils. Ground-up rocks alone do not provide everything a plant needs for long, healthy growth, though the soil you have made by pounding rocks will get your little plants started.

Now you can experiment to find out how sand, clay, and gravel can be made into rock.

Fill a clean glass about one-half full of coarse soil (soil with gravel and pebbles mixed in). Pour water into the jar and shake it hard. How does the water look now? Put the jar on your shelf and watch what happens. Do not touch the jar again. After it has stood for a day or so, the coarse material will settle to the bottom, and the water will be fairly clear. If all the water were to evaporate and then great pressure were applied to the layers of soil, the soil would be pressed firmly together. If the pressure continued for years and years (hundreds of thousands of years), the soil would harden into layers of rock. This is what happens to the sand and gravel and clay that is deposited in stream beds, lakes, and seas. Layer upon layer of rock is built up. This kind of rock is called sedimentary, because it is formed by sediment (bits of sand, clay, gravel or the remains of dead sea creatures). Sedimentary rock is always found in layers.

When it is formed from sand, it is called *sandstone*.

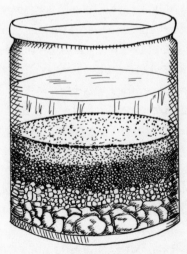

Sediment in layers

When it is formed from clay, it is called *shale*.

When it is made from pebbles cemented together with sand, it is called *conglomerate*.

When it is made from the ground-up shells and skeleton remains of sea creatures, it is called *limestone*.

There are other kinds of sedimentary rocks, but these are the most common. You should be able to find a sample of at least one of these in your own yard. Sedimentary rock is one of the three main kinds of rock in the earth's crust. In the next experiment you can discover more about the three main kinds of rock.

Go to a place where they make tombstones, or to a yard where they sell rock for stone masonry. Ask for some small scraps of different kinds of rock. You should be able to get samples of some of the following: granite, limestone, sandstone (usually sold as "flagstone"), slate, and marble. Perhaps you can also get some black lava rock and some light-colored pumice. You can usually find a piece of shale where there is excavating or road-building going on. It is rather soft rock in thin layers, and it smells like clay when you wet it.

When you get back to your laboratory, mark a cardboard box IGNEOUS ROCKS. In it put the granite pieces, the lava rocks, and the pumice.

On a second box write SEDIMENTARY ROCKS. Put your pieces of sandstone, limestone, and shale in this second box.

Mark a third box METAMORPHIC ROCKS. In this box go the pieces of marble and slate.

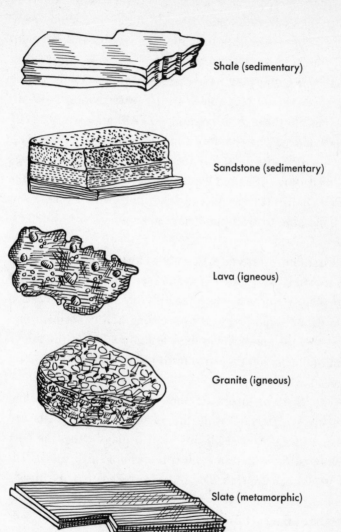

Shale (sedimentary)

Sandstone (sedimentary)

Lava (igneous)

Granite (igneous)

Slate (metamorphic)

Now you have the beginning of a rock collection. You may have several kinds of each of the specimens mentioned above. Granite, for instance, may be dark or light, and there is some granite that has a lovely pink color. The stone cutter may have chips of different kinds to give you. Sandstone, too, comes in different shades, from almost white through grays and pinks to almost red. Your limestone may be powdery white or it may be bumpy with the fossil shells of the sea creatures from which it was formed. What is called Texas limestone usually shows the fossil shells clearly. As you learn more about rocks, you will be able to trade and buy other pieces for your collection.

First, however, you will want to know a bit about these three kinds of rock — igneous, sedimentary, and metamorphic — and why they are different. This is a question you cannot answer by just observing and experimenting. To know the answer, you have to know some of the things that happened on the earth millions and millions of years ago.

The first, or original, rock came from hot, molten (melted) material inside the earth itself. Scientists are not sure what caused all this heat. It may be that the heat remained from the time when the whole earth was a ball of fiery hot material. The outside cooled, but the inside stayed hot. Or it may be that the great pressure from the weight of the earth's crust has caused enough heat to melt the rock material inside. Perhaps both of these explanations are true. We do know that the earth is hot enough deep, deep inside to melt solid rock. Melted rock is called magma.

Magma flows upward and sideways beneath the earth's crust. Sometimes there is a weak spot in the crust of the earth. In such a place, the pressure is less than in other places. Magma sometimes bursts through a weak pressure spot and erupts as a volcano. The magma (or lava, as the molten rock from a volcano is usually called) flows over the land and hardens rapidly, becoming volcanic or lava rock.

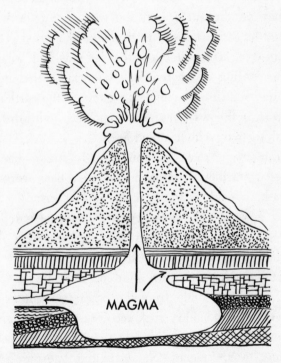

Most of the igneous rock of the world, however, was formed when masses of magma cooled inside the earth. As the magma moved slowly toward the earth's surface, it gradually cooled under the insulating rock of the outer crust. There, miles below the surface and yet well above the area of intense heat that lies deep within the earth, great masses of rock were formed. As the outer layers of the earth's crust have worn away, these igneous rock masses are exposed. Granite is such a rock. Any rock that was formed by the cooling of magma is igneous rock, whether on the surface of the earth where a volcano erupted or somewhere beneath the earth's crust. The important thing to remember is that igneous rock was made by the cooling of melted rock material called magma. You may want to remember the name of the earth's original rock in this way: *ignite* and *igneous,* both words have something to do with heat and fire.

Sedimentary rock, as you already know, has been formed from bits of sediment that have been worn away from older rocks by water, wind, and the grinding action of rock against rock. These sediments have been deposited in layers. Then great pressure for a great length of time has formed the loose sediment into hard rock.

Metamorphic, the third kind of rock in the earth's crust, has been made from the other two kinds. When igneous or sedimentary rock receives great pressure and heat over a long, long period of time, a complete change is made. "Meta" means "changed" and "morphic" means "form." Thus, heat and pressure have changed the following:

Granite (igneous) becomes gneiss (metamorphic)

Limestone (sedimentary) becomes marble (metamorphic)

Sandstone (sedimentary) becomes quartzite(metamorphic)

Shale (sedimentary) becomes slate (metamorphic)

All three kinds of rock — igneous, sedimentary, and metamorphic — may then be worn down by wind and water and other forces to form the sand, gravel, and clay that are the basis of soil. When decayed bits of plant and animal life are added, generation after generation, the soil that began as rock becomes rich and fertile, making it possible for plants, animals, and men to live on the earth's crust.

5

FOSSILS

Preserved inside some of the sedimentary rocks in the earth's crust are remains of plant and animal life. These remains are called fossils. There are probably no fossils in your back yard, but you may have seen some in a museum or in someone's rock collection. Or perhaps you have seen pictures of fossils in books or magazines. Fossils are important to scientists who study what the earth was like thousands and even millions of years ago.

To a scientist, a fossil is any trace or impression or remains of plant or animal life of long ago that has been preserved by burial in the earth's crust. It may be the imprint of a shell, the skeleton of a bird, the scales of a fish, the outline of a leaf, the track of a dinosaur, or the petrified limb of a tree. All of these belong to things that lived and died many, many, many years ago. By studying their traces in layers of rock, scientists discover what the earth was like in the past.

Often fossil remains of fish and sea shells are found on the desert or high and dry in the hills. Thus we know that once upon a time there was a sea where now there is dry land. When fossils of plants and animals that live only in hot climates are found in the rock layers of some cold country, we know that the climate there was not always cold. And, by studying the particular layer of rock that preserved the fossils, scientists can tell how long ago that hot period occurred and how long it lasted. It can be said that fossils give us an index to the history of the earth. By studying the fossils of plants and animals and comparing them with plants and animals of today, we can learn a great deal about the way living things have grown and developed and changed.

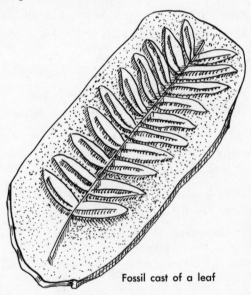

Fossil cast of a leaf

Fossil remains of dinosaurs from the age of reptiles are found in a layer of rock that contains clues to the kinds of plants and the many kinds of reptiles that lived in dinosaur times. The dinosaur period ended, and many other periods came and went before there were any traces of man on the earth. Thus we know not only how long ago

41

various animals and plants lived, but which ones lived together during the same age. We know these things from the earth's history in rock.

Here is an experiment to show you what kinds of fossils there are and how they were formed.

Put some damp clay into the bottom of a small cardboard box. Press a shell, a bone, or a seed pod into the clay, making a deep print. Remove the object and you have an empty mold. The *mold* is one kind of fossil. It is merely the impression of something that once had life but has long since disappeared.

Molds that are very flat are called *imprints*. They can be imitated by pressing leaves into soft clay. When the leaf is taken away, its imprint remains. Some imprints are just the footprints or tracks of prehistoric living things — tiny worm trails, huge dinosaur tracks, or the footprints of birds or mammals.

Often the fossil mold or imprint does not remain empty. It may be filled with some rock-forming material that makes an image of the original object. To see how

Imprint of a dinosaur foot

this works, take one of your empty clay molds. Mix a small amount of plaster of Paris with enough water to make it as thick as condensed milk. Mix it in a milk carton or clean tin can. Pour the mixture into the mold and let it set for several hours. When it is hard and solid, lift it out carefully. If you had a good mold to start with, you will have a good *cast*. The cast is another kind of fossil. Many fossils are casts, made in much the same way you made yours, but with different materials and slowly, over a period of many, many years.

Fossil cast of a shell

There is a different kind of fossil, which we call *petrified*. You may have seen pieces of petrified wood or bone. The process that makes things petrify is one you cannot imitate. Petrified wood is not wood that has been turned to stone, as many people say. Rather, it is wood that has been replaced by stone. As the tiny cells of the original wood disintegrated, each cell was replaced by a rock-forming chemical. This replacement happened so gradually, cell by cell, that the wood was perfectly remade in

43

rock. Even under a microscope some pieces of petrified wood look exactly like the structure of real wood.

If, by now, you have made fossil-like casts, imprints, and molds, you may want to buy a piece of petrified wood or bone to add to your collection of types of fossils.

Somewhere in your neighborhood you may be able to find some real fossils. Look around for places where road building, excavations, or streams have cut through layers of sedimentary rocks. You can usually see the different strata easily, like layers in a cake. The rock layers may be different in color — light gray, darker gray, almost black, tan, pink, or reddish. You may live near a quarry where sedimentary rock is cut for building purposes. There are quarries for sandstone or limestone in many parts of the country. If you do your fossil hunting around a quarry, be sure to have a grownup along, as quarries are usually dangerous and special care must be taken for safety.

If you do not know of a good place to find fossils, call or write to the nearest high school or college geology department for information. Geologists are usually familiar with the fossil beds in their areas. Fossils may be found in any sedimentary rock anyplace in the world. But they are naturally more plentiful in some places than in others.

Once you know where you are going on your fossil hunt, it is well to know what tools and equipment you should take with you. First of all, you will need a hammer and a chisel or pick. A regular geologist hammer is most useful, since it has the hammer part on one end and

44

the pick or chisel part on the other. Wear a heavy belt so you can hang your tools from it and keep your hands free in case you have to do some climbing. You will also need some old newspapers for wrapping any fossils you find and a heavy bag or canvas sack in which to carry them home.

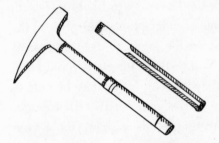

Geologist hammer and chisel

The technique of finding fossils in the rock layers is one you will have to learn by experience. Every collector has his own ways. They usually work something like this. When you find a layer of sedimentary rock (shale, sandstone, or limestone), pick out some small slabs. You may have to pry them out of the layer of rock. Split each slab open with your pick or chisel. Some split so easily that you can do it with your bare hands, nearly as easily as opening the pages of a book. Other rocks are harder, and you may have to hit hard with your chisel to make them split. Examine each slab of rock for traces of fossils. Look for tiny veins of leaves, traces of insects, imprints of shells, skeletons of fish. If you are careful in examining many layers of sedimentary rocks, your chances are good of finding some kind of fossil.

45

Another way of collecting fossil specimens is to go to a dealer who sells building stone. Ask him for scraps of Texas limestone, which is usually filled with shell fossils. He may also have other fossil rocks to show you or to sell you for a small price.

Some of the loveliest fossils ever known have been found in layers of coal. Coal fossils are likely to be imprints of ferns and leaves of other plants that grew in the lush tropical forests during the long-ago ages when coal was being formed. At one time these forests covered large areas of the earth. Your local coal dealer may be able to tell you more about the stories coal fossils tell. He may have some of these interesting fossils to show you or even to sell you.

If you are interested in building up a fossil collection of your own, you will find ways of exploring, collecting, buying, and trading with other fossil fans. You will also want to find out more about the many different plants and animals of the past that left their life history in the hard rock layers of the earth's crust.

Most of the fossils known today are of plants and animals that are now extinct — that is, their kind no longer exists. A few, however, have modern descendants that have kept many of the features of their prehistoric ancestors. They are sometimes called "living fossils" because they are living things that have come down to the present time without changing too much from their age-old ancestors, known to us by means of their fossil portraits in rock. Do you know any of these?

LIVING FOSSIL	PREHISTORIC ANCESTOR
Dragonfly. Now has a wing spread of eight inches.	Lived in the coal age. Then had a wing spread of twenty-nine inches.
Komodo. A large modern lizard.	Was one of the prehistoric reptiles in the dinosaur age.
Cockroach. Insect now found in houses.	Was the most common insect of the early coal age. Was then many times as large as now.
Garpike. A long, thin fish.	Lived 300,000,000 years ago in prehistoric seas.
Ginkgo tree. A common tree with flat, lobed leaves.	Grew abundantly in the lush forests of the age of reptiles.

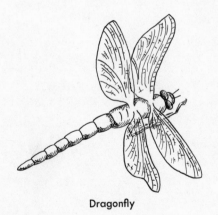

Dragonfly

Ginkgo leaves

Drawings or other pictures of any of the things listed in the left-hand column above would make an interesting addition to your fossil collection. Living fossils have family trees that go back millions and millions of years in the earth's history, with records preserved in the solid rock of the earth's crust.

6

WATER

Do you know how much of the earth's crust is covered by water? If you were to fly all around the world in all directions, looking from your plane window at every square mile, you could see only three-tenths of the earth's crust. The other seven-tenths is covered by water, the oceans of the world. Our five continents rise out of the continuous seas like five great islands. Where does all this water come from? What happens to the rain that falls on the continents? What happens to the rain that falls on your house and your yard? To find out more about the crust of the earth where you live, you will want to know something about water and some of the things it does, for water is a large and important part of the earth.

Rain that falls on the land cuts into solid rock, washes away loose soil, soaks through soft earth, drains downward in streams and rivers, and finally flows out into the ocean. Then the sun's rays on sea and land cause some of the water to rise into the air as water vapor. This is held in clouds and often carried for many miles over land and ocean until the air around the clouds cools enough to turn the vapor back to water once more. Then there is rain, and so the cycle continues over and over and over again.

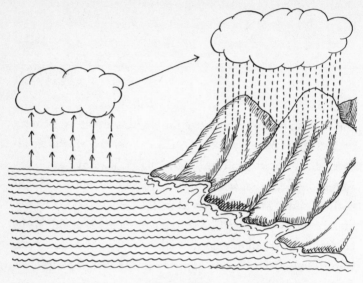

Water cycle

How much water do you have here in your yard? Perhaps there is a faucet and a hose for sprinkling. When you turn on the faucet, where does the water come from? Somewhere in the water cycle the water has been trapped and piped to your yard and your house. Perhaps your water comes from a well, or a mountain stream, or a river on its way to the ocean, or a lake or reservoir many miles away. Whatever its source, it is part of the wonderful cycle that keeps water continuously moving and continuously changing form.

Most materials of the earth can exist under certain conditions as solid, liquid, or gas. You already know that rock is liquid when it gets very, very hot deep inside the earth. If the melted rock becomes still hotter, it changes to gas. When the molten rock cools, it becomes a solid — solid rock, which makes up most of the earth's crust. Other kinds of matter can also change from solid to liquid to gas when there are great changes in the amount of heat. However, only water is commonly known and used in all three forms. Everybody knows solid water (ice), liquid water (the kind that rains), and water gas (water vapor such as fog or steam). In each of these forms, water serves us. Sometimes, when we cannot control it, water becomes a dangerous enemy. We need to know what water really is and why it behaves as it does.

This experiment will show how water changes from liquid to gas. On a sunny day, put the same amount of water into each of two wide-mouthed glass jars. Mark the exact water line on each jar with a strip of adhesive tape. Do not put the lids on the jars. Place one jar in a cool, shady place where the sun's rays cannot reach it. Place the other jar in the full sun all day long. In the evening, compare the amount of water left in each jar. The supply in each has diminished, but there is less water in the jar that stood in the sun all day than in the other. Where did the water go? We say that the water *evaporated*, that is, changed from liquid water to water vapor. Warm air helps water turn to vapor.

When you are in the kitchen, find out what happens when water boils. Put a half-cup of water in a teakettle and watch it boil. After a short while there will be no more water in the teakettle. What has happened to it? The same thing that happened to the water in the two jars outside, only much more quickly.

Now you have seen that water evaporates in the shade, in the sun, and over a fire. In which of the three cases did the evaporation occur most rapidly? Which took the longest?

Obviously, heat helps liquid water to turn to vapor. This explains the following statements:

Clothes dry faster in the sun than in the shade.

On sunny days the grass gets very dry.

Water evaporates from the bird bath in the yard.

The sun's rays lift moisture from the ocean.

The next experiment shows what happens when water changes from liquid to solid. (You will need your mother's permission and cooperation for this.)

Fill a glass peanut-butter jar with water. Fill it to the very top and screw the cap on tightly. Put the jar in a heavy paper bag and place it in the freezing compartment of your refrigerator or in your deep freezer. Leave it there for several days until it is frozen solid. Then take it out and see what has happened. Tear the bag open carefully because the glass jar will be broken. It broke because water in solid form (ice) takes more space than water in liquid form. It has enough force and power as it expands to break the glass. It can break materials that are even stronger than glass. You can picture what happens when water fills cracks in rocks and then freezes solid in winter. This behavior of water and ice makes many changes in the earth's crust.

Now you can do an experiment to show how water vapor and ice change to liquid. Put some wadded-up paper toweling in the bottom of a wide-mouthed glass jar. Pour some water onto the paper, just enough to soak it without making a pool of water. Be careful to keep the jar itself completely dry on the inside. Screw the cap on tightly so that no air or water vapor can escape. Then place the jar in the sun. You know from your first experiment that the heat of the sun will turn the water to vapor. Vapor is a colorless gas. You cannot see it. Next, get a few ice cubes from the refrigerator and put them in an aluminum foil pan. Place the pan on top of the jar. While the ice cubes are melting in the sun, inside the jar top tiny drops of water are forming. What is happening is simply that the top of the jar has become cooled. This in turn cools the water vapor in the jar to a temperature that changes it back to a liquid.

Heat {
   can change solid ice to liquid water
       and
    liquid water to vapor

Cold {
   can change water vapor to liquid
       and
    liquid water to ice

When there is a sudden spell of warm weather in late winter or early spring, what happens to the great snowbanks and rivers of ice? You can understand why there are sometimes terrible floods in the early spring.

In this experiment you will see how water changes the

face of the earth and how water damage can be prevented.

In a corner of your yard, or in sandbox if you have one, make a model of a section of land. Here are some features to include:

A hill, with ridges or gullies running up and down

A hill, with ridges or terraces running around

A valley or river bed between the hills

Some flat land planted with grass seed

Rocks, large and small

Some small pebbles on top of a mesa or plateau of sand

Tiny plants or trees along the river bed

A road of gravel with a bridge across the river bed

Anything else you can think of to make your model look like real farm land, mountains, valleys, forests, and meadows

To build your model, use ordinary soil, sand, gravel, and rocks of different sizes and colors. Put in some little plants (there are common weeds that make good miniature plants and trees). Then sow grass seed in the flat, low places. Sow more grass seed on the hill that has the terraces or ridges running around it. Leave the hill with the gullies unplanted. Do not plant the sand mesa, either. Water the grass seed and the plants every day until everything is growing well. By that time your model will look just like a real section of land. You may want to put some toy cars on the road, some little model houses and other buildings to represent farms or villages in the valleys, and some little people and farm animals in the fields.

Make your model look like a piece of America.

Then, when everything is in place and growing, begin to experiment with water. First, try a fine spray of rain (from the hose) over everything. Notice how the water drains. Now, let it rain harder and harder. Let it pour! Let the water fill up the river bed, rush down the gullies, soak into the farm land. Let it pour on top of the soft sand mesa. After you have made it rain hard for a long time, turn off the water and find out what has happened to the land. Of course, the rain may have come naturally rather than from your hose. If so, just wait till the rain has stopped and then study your model. Notice these things:

> Look at the bare hill with the gullies running up and down. Did the gullies become wider and deeper as the rain washed down? If so, where did the soil go?

> Look at the hill with the terraces. Did this hill wash away less than the bare hill? Did the ridges going around the hill seem to hold back some of the water? If a farmer plows a hilly field, is it better to have the furrows go around and around or up and down? Why?

> Look at the places with grass and other plants. Did the planted land wash away as easily as the bare land? How do plants hold on to the soil?

Look at the sand mesa with the pebbles scattered over its surface. Are some of the pebbles now resting on little platforms of sand? Was sand washed away between some of the pebbles? Do you see how pieces of hard rock on top of softer earth material causes strange-looking land surface?

Look at the river bed. Did the river overflow at any point? Was the river bed changed in any way? Was the bank of the river broken away?

Look at the road. Was soil washed across the road? Was the road damaged by the water? Were parts of the road swept away?

After you have studied all of these things on your earth model, build up your model until it looks as it did before the rain storm. As you work on this reconstruction, try to figure out how to protect the land from damage during another storm. Consider making these improvements:

Check-dams of wood (twigs), earth, and rock in the gullies and mountain streams

A protective wall along the river where it tends to overflow its banks

More planting to hold the soil

More terracing and "contour plowing" (furrows going around rather than up and down) to hold water on slopes long enough for it to soak into the ground

A dam in the main river to hold some of the water in a lake or reservoir for future use

Several reservoirs in the hills to catch and hold water for later use

You may think of other ways of changing your model by adding features that protect land against water damage. As you hear about storms and floods and the harm they do every year in the United States, think of some of the ways in which land can be protected. Try out your ideas on your back-yard model.

7

GRASS

Your back yard is probably like most yards in the United States. A large part of it is a grassy lawn. You walk on it, sit on it, play games on it, and stretch out on it to rest. Perhaps you also help to cut it, rake it, sprinkle it, reseed it, and feed it special chemicals to keep it strong and green. Most of the green plants in lawns are grasses. Do you know that grasses are the most important plants in the world?

There are very few places on the surface of the earth where grass of some sort cannot grow. The grass family is the most widespread of all plants. There are many different kinds of grass, and all of them are in some important ways like the little grass plants growing here in your lawn.

Directly or indirectly we are all dependent on grass for the most important foods we eat and the liquids we drink. Every day we use meat, eggs, milk, and other products from animals that feed on grass. Every day we also eat grass itself. Of course, we do not eat the whole plant the way cattle and sheep do, nor do we eat all kinds of grasses. But the seeds of certain grass plants form the main food for people all over the world. Rice, corn, wheat, rye, barley, and oats are grass plants whose seeds we eat.

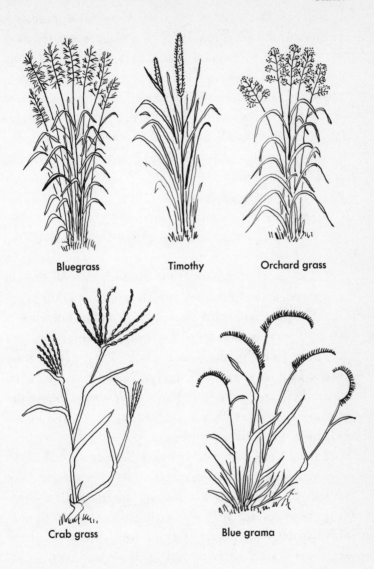

Bluegrass   Timothy   Orchard grass

Crab grass   Blue grama

Here are the ways to tell whether or not a plant is a member of the grass family. Find a place where the lawn has not been cut recently. There may be some tall grass around a tree, under a bush, or at the edge of the yard where the lawn mower cannot reach. Dig up a couple of these grass plants and wash off all the dirt. Put the plants into a clear glass filled with water. Study the roots, the stems, the leaves. Use your hand lens to see the details. Look for these things:

Stems with solid joints

One leaf at each joint

Each leaf set on the side of the stem opposite the leaf below

Two parts of each leaf: the sheath, which fits around the stem, and the blade, which is long and thin

Flowers that are tiny and growing on fine branches

All true grasses have these five characteristics. Can you find them on the plants in your glass? Try different grass plants. Pull off some of the leaves. Notice how neatly the sheath fits around the stem like a hollow tube. Study the ribbon-like blade with fine ridges running up and down. Do any of your grass plants have flowers?

If there are no grasses in flower in your yard, look in a vacant lot or field for grass that has been uncut long enough for the plants to produce flowers. Collect some grass flowers. Not very showy, are they? Grass flowers are not noted for their beauty or fragrance. Still, there are some grass flowers that are delicate and dainty and really quite pretty. Find some that you like. Look at them

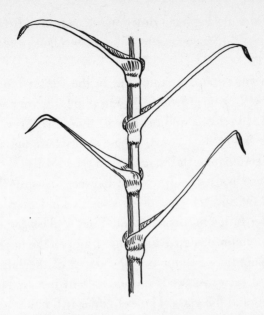

through your hand lens. Do you see any powdery pollen? Do you see any tiny grass seeds? A grass plant, when it is mature, produces flowers that make seeds for new plants.

This experiment will show how lawn grass grows from seed. You can do this indoors as well as outdoors. It is a good indoor experiment for the winter. Wet a piece of sponge or sponge rubber and put it on an old plate or an aluminum-foil pie pan. Take about a teaspoonful of lawn grass seed and sprinkle it over the sponge. Keep the sponge damp and watch what happens in a few days.

As soon as the tiny grass seeds have begun to sprout, pick off one each day and study it with your hand lens. Make a drawing every two days and keep a record of the

61

growth of a grass plant. How long does it take from seed to first signs of sprouting to a complete plant, with roots, stem, and leaves?

Keep your sponge damp and in the sun and see how long it will keep growing. Do the plants in your experiment look as strong and healthy as those that grow in the soil? Probably not. Your sponge plants lack the animal and vegetable material that enriches good soil.

You can learn the difference between the growth of a grass plant and the growth of another kind of plant by doing the following experiment. Line a glass jar with a piece of blotter or paper toweling. Dampen the paper and put a spoonful of water on the bottom of the jar. Now, put about six grass seeds on one side of the jar between the paper and the glass. The wet paper will hold the seeds in place if you are careful. Now you will need some seeds of corn and beans. Seed corn can be bought in a small envelope at a nursery, a feed store, or at the seed counter in your local dime store. Dried beans (navy, pinto, lima, or other kinds) are probably in your own kitchen. If not, you can buy them at a grocery store. Or, you can buy seed beans where you buy the corn.

On the side of the jar opposite the grass seeds, place two corn seeds and two bean seeds, between the blotter and the glass. Keep all the seeds about halfway between the top and the bottom of the jar.

On one side of your jar you have a row of regular grass seeds. On the other side you have four other seeds. The corn seeds are actually grass seeds, too. The bean seeds are from another kind of plant. Beans are not members of the grass family.

Keep the paper in your jar moist but not soggy wet. Watch your seeds sprout and grow into little plants. The corn plants grow to look like the grass plants. They each send up a stem and a single blade as they start to grow. But the bean plants grow differently from the grasses. Each bean plant sends up a stem and two little leaves.

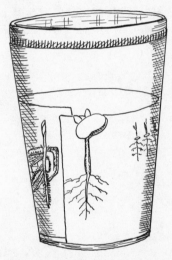

Corn, bean, and grass sprouts

Since prehistoric times, people have eaten food made from seeds of grass plants. Cereals, breads, and some of the other common foods we eat today are made largely from grain, as the edible grass seeds are called. How many food products made from grain can you find in your kitchen? Read the labels on packaged foods. The ingredients are usually listed. For instance, on a package of macaroni, the label reads, "Made from finest wheat flour. . . ." Look at the labels on breakfast foods, noodles, soups, instant puddings, cookies, crackers, and different kinds of bread and rolls. How many products can you find for each of the following grains?

Oats   Rice

Wheat   Barley

Corn   Rye

All of these are from common cereal grasses. Collect samples of as many of these grains as you can find at

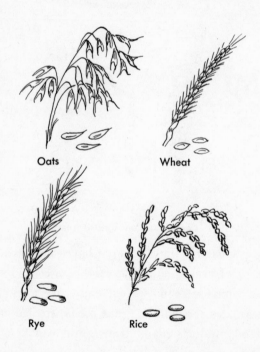

Oats   Wheat

Rye   Rice

home. In your kitchen you may have rolled oats, cracked wheat, white (wheat) flour, corn meal, whole corn for popping, white or brown rice, and pearl barley. In these foods the cereal grains have been cracked, parched, bleached, ground, or otherwise treated to make the seeds good for eating.

To get cereal seeds that will grow into cereal grass plants, you will have to go to a seed store and buy some, or get some from a farmer friend. Try to get about a cupful of each kind because there are three different things you can do with them.

First, make an exhibit of different kinds of cereal seeds. A few seeds of each kind in a small cellophane bag can be fastened to a card and labeled.

Second, make an experimental garden in flowerpots or tin cans with holes punched in the bottom for drainage. You can do this experiment outdoors when the weather is warm, or indoors any time of the year. Fill each pot or can with fine garden soil. Be sure that there are no lumps or rocks in the soil you use. For best results, sift the soil through a strainer or piece of metal screen. Otherwise, rub the soil fine with your hands before putting it into the cans. Fill to about an inch from the top. Use one can or pot for each kind of grain.

Soak the seeds you are going to plant — five or six of a kind will be enough — for an hour or more in warm water. Use a separate cup for each kind of seed to avoid getting your seeds mixed up. Soaking will soften the hard outer shells and make the seeds sprout more easily. After the seeds have been soaked, plant them in separate pots. Plant the corn seeds about one inch deep. Plant the other seeds about a half-inch deep. Keep the soil always damp but never muddy. Label each pot with the name of the grain planted in it. As your plants grow, watch them carefully and notice ways in which they are alike and ways in which they are different. Soon you may be able to tell the young plants apart without looking at the labels.

Third, try ways of making food from cereal seeds. Take one kind of grain at a time. Find a large flat rock and a round rock small enough to hold in your hand. Scrub the rocks with soapy water. Rinse them well with a hose and leave them in the sun to dry. When the rocks are thoroughly dry, put a handful of wheat grains on top of the flat rock. Grind them as fine as you can with the round rock. Brush the ground grain into a clean wire strainer or sieve. Shake it over a clean pan. The part that falls through the sieve is wheat flour. The coarse bits that stay in the sieve are bran. If you mix your stone-ground flour with enough water to make a thick paste or dough and add a few grains of salt, you can make a flat pancake that you can bake in an oven or in a dry frying pan over a low fire. This is a simple kind of bread.

Take another kind of grain and pound it fine with your grinding rock. Sift the flour through your sieve, add water enough to make a thin paste, and a pinch of salt. Then cook it slowly until it gets thick and bubbly. Taste a little of it. Add sugar and cream. Does it taste something like the hot cereals you sometimes have for breakfast? Try different ways of grinding, pounding, soaking, cooking, and baking the cereal grains. These are some of the ways man has made food from the seeds of grasses for thousands and thousands of years.

Here is an experiment to show how grass helps save the soil. Take a hike around your neighborhood. Look at all the spots where the earth is bare. Notice slopes, hillsides, and stream banks where no grass is growing. Notice how heavy rains have washed away the soil. Wind picks up bare soil, too, and blows it away. Think of the earth model you made when you were studying about water. Grass plants prevent the wearing away (or erosion) of land.

Food for animals and food for people; lawns for comfort, fun, and beauty; and networks of roots and stems and blades keeping precious topsoil from blowing or washing away! All this, and more, we owe to the large family of little green plants we call the grasses!

8

FLOWERS

Look around your yard and count the different kinds of flowers. You may have roses and pansies and lilies and dandelions and white clover and many others. Or, you may look carefully and think there are no flowers at all. That is because you are looking for only the gay, beautiful blossoms we think of first when we say "flowers." But if there is anything green growing in your yard, any bushes, trees, grasses, weeds, or plants of any kind, there are flowers in your yard sometime during the spring or summer.

Every kind of plant that can be grown from seed has flowers sometime during its life. Flowers are so much enjoyed for their beauty and their fragrance that we sometimes make the mistake of thinking that their main purpose is to give us pleasure. Actually, flowers do something much more important and much more wonderful. It is only in a flower that seeds can be made. Flowers make it possible for new plants to grow through production and distribution of seeds. The beauty of a flower, its form and color and perfume, all help in the flower's main work, seed-making.

Where and how does a flower make seeds? Find some kind of large flower. A lily, a tulip, or some other large, open blossom is best. Lay it carefully on a piece of cardboard. With a single-edge razor blade, or with a very sharp knife, cut the flower in half lengthwise. This will give you a cross-section view of the important parts of a flower. Find the different parts and then make a diagram of them. The list below tells you what the different parts are and where to look for them.

Pistil. This is usually a long, thin tube right in the middle of the flower. It has a little platform at the top and a fat place at the bottom.

Ovary. This is the fat place at the bottom of the pistil. If you have sliced through the ovary, you will see that it is filled with tiny round things that look like seeds. They may not be seeds yet, but they can become seeds if certain things happen.

Ovules. These are the tiny round things you noticed in the ovary at the bottom of the pistil.

Stamens. Stamens usually grow in a circle around the pistil. They are tubes, each with a soft, fuzzy head.

Anther. This is the fuzzy head at the top of each stamen. Touch the anthers with your fingers. What happens? Does something rub off on your fingers?

Pollen. This is the soft powder on the anthers. It is pollen that came off on your fingers.

The pistil and the stamens are the seed-making parts of a flower. They look different in different kinds of flowers, but in all flowers the pistil, with its case of ovules at the bottom, and the stamens, with their pollen at the top, serve the same purpose. Pollen cannot grow into

69

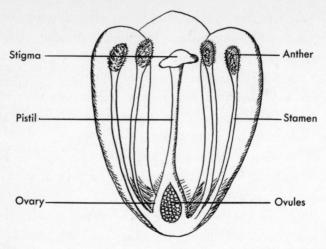

seeds by itself, nor can the little ovules alone become seeds.

1. Pollen from the anthers of stamens reaches the top of a pistil. The pollen may be blown by the wind or carried by insects from one flower to another or from stamens to pistil of the same flower.

2. From each grain of pollen that reaches a pistil, a long, slim tube grows down the pistil and right into the ovary.

3. When one of the pollen tubes strikes an ovule in the ovary, it pierces it. The scientist says that the ovule has now been "fertilized."

4. Now, and only now, can the ovule grow into a seed. Many grains of pollen can pierce or

fertilize many ovules. In this way, a single flower can make a great number of seeds.

After you have studied your first large flower and learned its different seed-making parts, collect other flowers, large and small. Remove the petals of some and find the stamens and pistils. Cut some more of them as you did the first one and find the place where the ovules lie, ready to be fertilized, or already fertilized and growing into seeds. Notice how one kind of flower differs from another in size and shape and arrangement of stamens and pistils. Yet all of them have the same job to do — to make seeds that can grow into new plants.

Find a place in your yard or somewhere else near home where there are a number of plants in bloom. Watch closely and wait until a bee or a butterfly, moth or other flying creature, visits the flowers. Keep track of the way the insect travels from flower to flower.

To know what the insect is after as it goes from blossom to blossom, pull off a flower and suck the end of it. It will taste sweet. A honeysuckle blossom has much sweetness, but other flowers have enough to be noticed. This sweetness is the nectar, which is deep inside the flower.

To reach the nectar, the visiting insect must dive down into the flower, past the stamens and pistil. Pollen from the stamens clings to the insect's body. Some of the pollen then rubs off on the pistils as the insect dips into different flowers in search of nectar. This is one of nature's won-

71

derful ways of making sure that the ovules are fertilized so they can grow into seeds.

Pollination by insect visitors is so important that farmers sometimes rent hives of bees to help pollinate the blossoms of their fruit trees. But even without the help of insects there are ways in which plants spread their pollen.

Collect several stems of grass that have long, fuzzy flowers. Look at them through your hand lens. Can you see the tiny little blossoms on the flower heads? Hold them over a piece of dark paper and shake them gently. Blow on them, too, and see what happens. Some pollen will probably fall on the paper. When the wind blows, it can carry pollen from place to place. Thus, even if no insects visit these flowers, the pollen can be distributed, and some of it will reach the pistils of other grass flowers. In this way wind helps pollination.

Take more samples of pollen-covered grass flowers.

Shake them over a pan of water. You will find that the pollen is light enough to float. What do you think happens when pollen falls or is blown into a stream? Since it floats, pollen from one plant can be carried great distances by water and then washed ashore against other plants. Water, as well as wind and insects, helps to pollinate flowers. These are the three main ways in which nature carries pollen from one flower to another.

Now that you know that a flower is an important part of nearly every kind of plant, you will be able to make an interesting collection whether you have a flower garden or not. Here are some suggestions for making different kinds of flower collections:

Flowers from common grasses

Flowers from weeds

Flowers from bushes

Flowers from trees

Wild flowers (from fields, roadsides, woods, deserts, mountains)

Flowers from food plants (tomatoes, radishes, onions, cucumbers, lettuce, etc.)

Flowers from your flower garden

There are many ways of arranging flower collections. Here are a few ideas to get you started.

A living flower collection. Take some small glass or plastic pill bottles. Cut round holes in a cardboard box (a candy box or a shoe box will do) and stand the pill bottles in the holes. This makes a convenient rack that will hold from six to twelve specimens at a time. Fill the

73

bottles with water and put one kind of flower in each. Try to show each kind of flower in several stages, one blossom fully opened, one or two partly opened, and several buds. Include a bit of stem and a leaf or two if possible. If you know the name of the plant, write it on a little card and fasten it to the front of the bottle with a bit of Scotch tape. You might keep a collection of this kind going all summer, changing the flowers and adding new ones as they come into bloom. Wild-flower collections in the museums of our national parks are often exhibited in much this way.

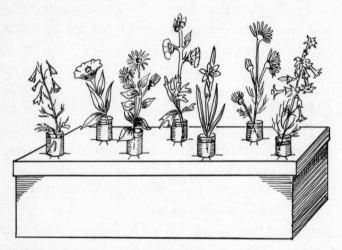

A pressed flower collection. Graceful, slender-stemmed flowers that are not too thick and solid are best for pressing. Pick your specimens and spread them carefully between several layers of newspaper cut into quarter-sheet size. Keep adding layers of papers and flowers, making sure to have three or four thicknesses of paper between flower layers. Place the whole stack on a flat box or table and put a board and a brick or about a dozen large magazines on top. The weight will press the flowers as the soft newspaper soaks up the moisture.

After a few days, look at your specimens. The flowers will be flat and soft but not yet dry. Move them carefully to dry papers. Arrange the stems, flowers, and leaves exactly as you want them to be when they are completely dried. Stack up the layers again, put the weights back on top, and forget about them for several weeks. By then your specimens should be completely dry. They will not look very much like living flowers, but they will have a delicate, fairy-like beauty and pale, silvery colors.

Mount your pressed flowers on cards cut from a sheet of black flocked paper. Tiny drops of transparent cement will hold the dried flowers to the paper. Cover each card with a sheet of thin plastic or cellophane and seal the edges with Scotch tape. The flocked paper, which looks like black velvet, and the plastic can be bought at a stationery store. Neither of them is expensive. One large sheet of each can be cut into many flower mounts.

Each specimen mount should have a label on the back or on the front. Write the name of the flower, when and where you found it, facts about the family to which it belongs, and any other information you may have about the specimen. Gummed labels, carefully written in ink, look neat and are easy to use.

Once mounted, your collection will last indefinitely. It will be both artistic and impressive. By arranging groups of weeds, grasses, and wild flowers into a single composition, you can make a flower picture that can be framed and used as an unusual gift.

A 3-D flower collection. To preserve both the shape and the color of flowers, you will need some fine white sand and a number of cardboard boxes. Pansies, dogwood, daffodils, and other sturdy flowers are good for this method of preservation. First, pour a thin layer of sand on the bottom of a box. A one-pound candy box is just the right size. Next, place several fresh flowers on top of the sand. Then, carefully and slowly, cover the flowers with more sand. Place the box in the sun. Keep it from being shaken and do not let it get wet. In two or three weeks your flowers will be ready. You can speed up the drying process by keeping your box of sand and flowers in the oven for twenty-four hours. The heat from the pilot light will dry the flowers. Pour the sand off gently, for the dry flowers are very fragile. If your sand drying has been done carefully, the flowers will keep their original shape and color.

Mount each specimen on the bottom of a small cardboard box. You may want to paint the inside of the box black before you put the flower in. A black background will make the flower show up well. Fasten the flower with drops of clear cement. Then cover the top of the box with plastic or cellophane and write your identification label on the back. A 3-D collection is an exceptionally beautiful way of keeping a permanent record of the flowers you collect around your home area.

An original picture flower collection. This is an easy
and effective way of keeping track of the flowers that
grow in your neighborhood. You need one sheet of ordinary drawing paper for each kind of flower. Choose a
flower you are interested in. Using regular wax Crayolas,
make a careful drawing of the flower, its buds, leaves,
and stems. Put the color on heavily and make your picture large and bright. If your flower is white, use the
white Crayola even though it does not show up now on the
light paper. Later, as you will see, it will show up beautifully. In fact, the light colors will be more effective
than the dark ones. When your crayon drawing is fin-
ished, you are ready for the next step.

For this you will need some black water-color paint.
Any kind will do — tempera, poster paint, calcimine, or
the black from your box of water colors. Take a soft

brush and use the paint as black as you can get it. Paint all over the page, drawing and all. Watch what happens. You will find that all the bare spaces on the paper will hold the black paint. But every place where you have made crayon marks will resist the black paint and show up brightly against the black background. The result will be a dramatic colored picture like a print. You can make lovely nature prints with this crayon-resist method.

Whatever method you choose for keeping a record of the flowers you see, you will have fun looking through the grass and weeds and bushes for interesting new specimens. As you look at each flower, remember that it is not just something pretty to look at or to smell. It is far more important than that. It is part of nature's scientific machinery for the making of seeds that are necessary to grow new plants.

9

PLANTS FROM SEEDS

Every flower, vegetable, bush, vine, and tree in your yard started with a little seed. Practically all of the plants on the earth began with seeds. Kernels of corn grow into corn plants, acorns into oak trees, and from tiny seeds as small as grains of sand have grown many of the flowers and weeds you see around you. Somewhere inside every seed there is the beginning of a plant. When a seed is given food, water, and warmth, it opens up and the baby plant begins to grow. Then, if conditions are right, the tiny plant grows into an adult plant that bears flowers and makes seeds, and the process begins all over again. This is going on right now in your yard.

As you have already found out, wheat, corn, barley, rye, oats, and other cereal foods are the seeds of grasses. You also eat many kinds of beans, peas, and nuts, which are the seeds of other kinds of plants. Some of these plants are small and bushy. Some are vines. Others are large trees. All grow from seeds.

Most seeds grow in special containers, which protect the young seeds until they are ripe. Then, in many wonderful ways, the seeds reach places where they can grow into new plants. Beans and peas grow in pods. So do the seeds of most garden flowers. Some seeds, especially nuts, grow inside hard shells. Others are protected within the fleshy or juicy fruit of the mother plant. When the fruit is ripe, it falls to the ground. The fleshy part rots away or is eaten by birds or animals, and the seed remains.

Of the millions and millions of seeds produced each year, only a small number actually develop into new plants. Many are eaten or otherwise destroyed. Others never reach the kind of place where there is enough warmth, moisture, and food to make them grow. But since each plant produces many, many seeds, there are always some that will grow into new plants.

Here is a list of some common foods that have seeds in them. You may know of others to add to the list.

Orange	Tomato	Date
Apple	Strawberry	Grapefruit
Squash	Grape	Plum
Avocado	Green bean	Lemon
Melon	Cherry	Eggplant
Cucumber	Pear	Cranberry

How many of these do you think are fruits? From a scientific point of view, every one of the foods listed above is a fruit, because each contains the plant's seeds. The fruit was preceded by a flower. The flower produced seeds. The flower then dropped off. The seed container and the seeds continued to grow. The seed container is the fruit of the plant.

Some of the fruits listed above are eaten, seeds and all. In others, we remove the seeds first or eat around them. The seeds we eat will of course not grow into new

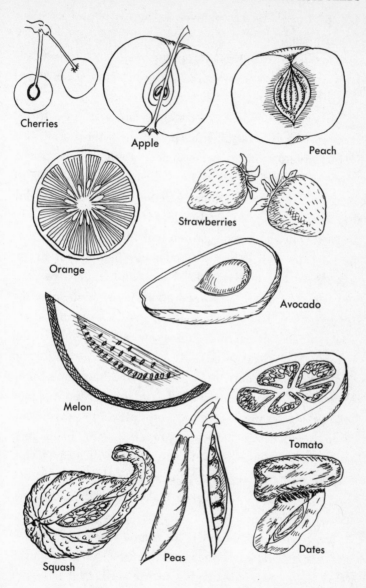

Cherries

Apple

Peach

Orange

Strawberries

Avocado

Melon

Tomato

Squash

Peas

Dates

plants. But those we remove can be saved and used for experiments.

Here is an experiment you can make to find out how long it takes for a new plant to grow from seeds found in fruits.

Collect the seeds from different kinds of raw fruits. You may want to begin with some of the following: grapefruit, tomato, squash, watermelon, apple, plum, peach, orange. Wash the seeds and dry them in the sun. Some of them will be small. Others will be large. But each one has the beginnings of a baby plant inside.

Next, put some good garden soil into small flowerpots or tin cans with holes punched in the bottom for drainage. Plant two to six seeds of one kind in each of your pots or cans. Plant each seed about twice as deep as the seed is wide. Keep them watered and in a warm, sunny spot. Some will sprout and grow more quickly than others. The citrus seeds (from oranges, lemons, and grapefruit) will not start growing for a long time. Keep a record of the date each kind is planted. Find out how many days or weeks it takes your plants to get started. If the weather gets cold while you are waiting, bring your pots indoors. Some of your fruit plants will make lovely kitchen gardens all through the winter. Shiny deep green plants from grapefruit seeds make especially attractive indoor gardens.

The next experiment will show how a new plant grows inside a seed. The best seeds for this experiment are large dried lima beans. Remember to use seeds that have not been cooked. Soak the beans overnight to soften the outer skins. Take one bean and carefully split it open. Look at the halves through your hand lens. Can you see the baby plant curled up at the end of one half? Repeat this with several beans until you can draw a diagram showing how the baby plant looks inside the seed. You will notice that only a small part of the large seed is the new plant. The rest of the seed is the food that the new plant will need in its early stages of growth. Later, when roots and leaves have developed, the plant will be able to get its food from outside sources.

Take an old glass and put a piece of blotting paper or several layers of paper towel on the bottom. Put some water in the glass. Let it stand for a few minutes until the paper has soaked up as much water as it can hold. Then pour off the water, leaving the wet paper in the glass. Put three or four of your lima beans on the wet paper. Wait a few days and see what happens. Make a record of the date when the roots appear. How long after does the stem appear? How long does it take until the baby plant inside the seed has grown into a true plant with roots, stem, and leaves? When this happens, you can remove your sprouting beans from the glass and plant them carefully in some soft soil. If you plant them in your garden, space them about a foot apart. If you do your planting in flowerpots or cans, you will need one container at least as big as a two-pound coffee can for each bean plant. Be sure there are drainage holes in the bottom of each can. With good soil and enough sun and water, the bean sprouts should grow into healthy plants. If you take care of them, you can raise them through their complete growth cycle, from seeds to young plants and then to plants with flowers, seeds, and seed pods or fruits. If you want to, you can then do the experiment all over again next year, using your own home-grown seeds.

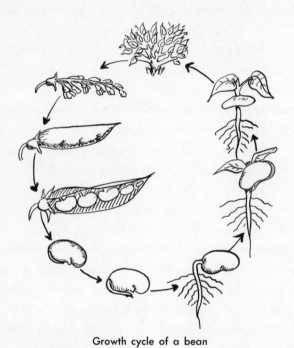

Growth cycle of a bean

In the following experiment you will learn where and how you find seeds and seed pods. You will have to do some exploring, some collecting, and some scientific detective work. In most parts of the United States it is best to begin this science adventure late in summer or early in the fall when plants have their seed-making well under way.

Collect seeds and their containers from every plant in your yard. Find others in fields or vacant lots near home. Naturally, the kinds of plants and seeds you find depend on the climate where you live. You may be able to collect the long slim pods of the California poppy, or you may find a chestnut tree with its soft-lined burs. Wherever you live, you can look for dandelions, weeds, and wild grasses. Where there are plants with flowers, there will be seeds and seed pods. Collect samples of as many kinds as you can find. Egg cartons, with twelve separate spaces in each, are good places to keep the seed pods you collect. Here are a few suggestions of what to look for as you make your collection of seed pods:

White-headed dandelions
Milkweed pods
White clover
Yellow mustard weed
Wild grasses
Rose bushes with fat, red hips
Honeysuckle vines after the flowers have dropped
Cattails
Tumbleweed
Garden flowers that have gone to seed — zinnias, four-o'clocks, poppies, nasturtiums, sunflowers, asters, sweet peas, impatience
Garden vegetables that have gone to seed — onions,

radishes, lettuce, cabbage

Trees, with their special seeds

Oak — acorns

Maple — seeds with wings

Nut trees with their nuts (walnut, hickory, piñon, hazel)

These are only a few suggestions to start you off. You will discover more as you search.

Every plant has been provided by nature with a way of getting its seeds away from the mother plant to some other place where they can grow independently. Here are a few of the ways seeds travel. See how many different kinds you can find near home.

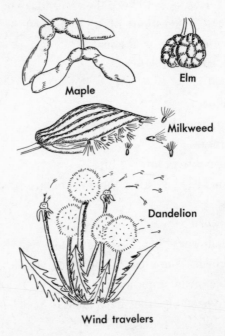

Maple

Elm

Milkweed

Dandelion

Wind travelers

Dandelion, thistle, milkweed, cattail, and others have their own little parachutes. Watch how easily one of these seeds floats through the air when you blow it. The seeds of maple and elm trees have glider wings. They are heavier than the parachute seeds, but their wings help them to sail far in the breeze. Still others, like some of the grass seeds, are so fine and light that the wind just blows them away.

Coconut, the world's biggest seed, floats easily when it falls into a stream, lake, or ocean. The American lotus plant grows its seeds in a boatlike pod that bobs along on top of the water.

Foxtail, burdock, sticktight, cocklebur, beggar's-lice, and other prickly plants have barbed seed pods that cling to the fur of animals. Have you ever had to pull any of these out of your socks or sweater after playing in a field or vacant lot?

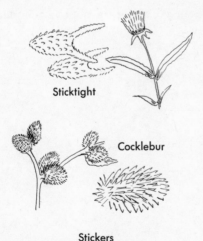

Sticktight

Cocklebur

Stickers

Nuts, fruits, berries, and grains are picked up by different kinds of animals. Chipmunks, squirrels, birds, and field mice take these seeds from the plants and run or fly away with them. Some are hidden in nests. Some are eaten. And some are dropped along the way. Man is one of the animals that scatter such seeds far and wide. He eats fruits like peaches, plums, and cherries and throws away the seeds. Some of these seeds grow into new plants. Man also gathers seeds and stores them for future planting. Seeds are sold commercially and are shipped all over the world. Man's seed-gathering and seed-planting activities are responsible for the spread of many kinds of plants.

Certain plants have seed pods designed so perfectly that, when the seeds are ripe, the slightest touch makes the pod snap open and shoot out the seeds. Some of these plants are wood sorrel, jewelweed, touch-me-not, witch hazel, impatience, California poppy, genesta, and moun-

Impatience, a seed-shooter

tain broom. If you find any of these in your neighborhood, you will have fun experimenting with them.

You may wonder what happens to all the seeds that are blown or carried away. Here is a way of finding out about some of them. Fill a flowerpot with some good topsoil from your yard. Water it until it is damp all the way through but not muddy. Then put a large glass jar over it, upside down. You have now made a little hothouse for

your experiment. Keep the pot in the sun and watch what happens. Remember, you begin with plain, damp soil. You will see, each day, that the water vapor from the soil will condense to drops of water on the inside of the jar. This should keep the soil always moist. The sun will keep

89

it warm. In a week or less you may find tiny plants beginning to grow from your "bare" soil. How did they get started? What must have been in the soil to start the baby plants? Keep the pot moist and warm long enough to find out how many different kinds of seeds must have been in your pot of garden soil.

Try the experiment several times, using soil from different places. You know now how the seeds may have reached the soil and why weeds grow in gardens and in the farmers' fields. There are plants nearly everywhere there is soil. And most of them begin and end with seeds.

10

PLANTS FROM SPORES

In your search for flowers and seeds in your neighborhood, you may have made some important discoveries. Some plants never have flowers at all. And not all plants are green. Have you found any mushrooms, toadstools, or puffballs? They are plants. Yet they have no flowers, no leaves, no green color. Have you discovered any mosses, ferns, or horsetails? They are green and they are plants, but they, too, never have flowers. No flowers means no seeds. How, then, can such plants reproduce?

Fortunately, nature has given these flowerless and seedless plants a special way of making new plants. Baby plants grow from things called spores, which are produced by the adult plants. Spores are something like seeds but differ in several ways. For one thing, a spore is much, much tinier than any seed you have ever seen. A single spore is so small that it can be seen only through a powerful microscope. One plant can produce millions or even more than a billion spores in one season. Many, many spores grow together in each little spore case. When the spores are ripe, the spore case usually pops open, and the fine, powdery spores are blown and scattered far and wide.

Only a few of the billions of spores in the air ever

have a chance to grow into new plants. Those that do are the few that happen to land where there is moisture, warmth, and food.

Spore plants are not as important as seed plants. In the long ago prehistoric ages of the earth's history, most of the plants grew from spores. Plants with flowers and seeds came later. They were a big improvement over the spore plants. Reproduction by means of seeds is more efficient and less wasteful. Today there are many more seed plants than spore plants. Yet spore plants are interesting to know about. Some are pretty to look at, some are a nuisance, some are deadly poison if eaten, and many of them are valuable for the special jobs they do.

Some of the spore plants you can find are green. All green plants can make their own food. The green color is from chlorophyll, the chemical in plants that turns air and water into food. Sunlight furnishes the energy for this food-making process, which is called photosynthesis. Many of the spore plants, however, are not green. They contain no chlorophyll and so cannot manufacture their own food. Mushrooms, toadstools, lichens, and other fungus plants are examples. They live off the food made by other plants. They grow inside living or dead plant material and get their nourishment from it. Mold is another kind of spore plant that grows in this way.

Ferns, mosses, mushrooms, toadstools, fungi, lichens, and molds, all are plants. They do not look much alike and they grow in different places and in different ways. Yet they are all alike in one important respect. They all make new plants from spores rather than from seeds.

To find out how spores grow on ferns, look for some ferns in the shady corners of your yard. If you can, find some different kinds in a park or in the woods. Remember as you look at ferns that plants like these have been growing on the earth for millions of years, long, long before any flowering plants existed. The feathery leaf stems of ferns are called *fronds*. Examine the underside of a frond and you will see rows of tiny brown or yellow dots. These are the spore cases of the fern plant. Each of these tiny cases holds many, many spores. When they are ripe, they will fall to the ground or be blown into the air. A few of them will grow into new fern plants. Collect some leaves from different kinds of ferns. Study the spore cases with your hand lens. Notice how tightly the spore cases stick to the leaves. Try to scrape off some of the larger

93

ones. If the spore case breaks open, you will see the spores, hundreds of them. But they will look like a bit of powder. Even through your hand lens you cannot see the separate spores.

You will want to find out also how the spores grow on mosses. If you live near the woods, you should be able to find some green mosses. Pry up a few chunks and carry them home in a tin can. You will also need a can of rich woodsy soil from the same place where you found the moss. Now you are ready to make a little moss garden that will last all winter if you give it the right care. Here is how to do it.

Take a large glass pickle jar, two-quart or one-gallon size. Lay it on its side in a shallow box or tray of sand. The side lying in the sand is now the bottom. Put some sand and pebbles (about $\frac{1}{2}$ inch deep) inside the jar. Cover this drainage layer with enough of your woodsy soil to make a planting level as high as the opening of the jar. Add a few interesting small rocks. Then plant the pieces of moss by pressing the underside of each into the soil. Water the garden and screw the cover on the jar. Keep it in a shady place and watch it every day. If it seems too soggy wet, leave the jar cover off for a few hours. This will allow some of the water vapor to escape from the jar. It will also admit fresh air into the garden. You will soon learn just how much moisture and air your garden needs. Usually moss will grow well in a garden of this kind for many months without needing any extra water if you keep the lid screwed on. The water cycle will

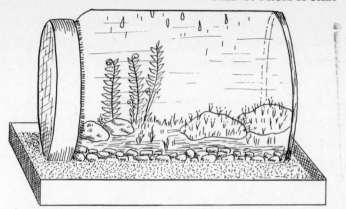

work within the jar. Keep watching your moss plants through your hand lens. Notice the tiny spore cases growing on slender stems. If conditions are right, new moss plants will grow from some of these spores, right here in your pickle-jar garden.

Another experiment will show you how spores grow on mushrooms and toadstools. Look in the lawns, gardens, fields, and woods around home. Find some place where mushrooms, toadstools, puffballs, or other kinds of non-green plants are growing. Remember, some of these are deadly poison if eaten. Even a small bite could kill a person. But they are not poisonous to touch. The best way to study them is to look at them carefully while they are growing in the ground. The main part of the plant is underground. It is a network of light threads, spread out and feeding on the dead plant and animal material in the soil. The parts of the plant that you see are the stem of the spore case and the "cap," which is the spore case itself.

Toadstools. Look at the underside of an open cap. Notice the fine ribs. Between these ribs are the spores. When the spores are ripe, they will fall out like dry powder. Some of them will grow into new toadstools.

Mushrooms. If you cannot find any toadstools growing in your yard, you can get a few mushrooms at a grocery store. Look inside the cap (the spore case) and find the place where the spores grow.

Mushrooms and toadstools

Puffballs. The spore cases of puffballs do not open up like little umbrellas as the toadstool caps do. They stay round and shut until the spores are ripe. Then the cap dries up, and when a person or animal steps on it, the cap bursts open and the black spore powder puffs out. Find a dry puffball and squeeze it, and you will see how it works.

96

Here is an experiment to show how molds grow. Molds are plants similar to mushrooms and toadstools, but much, much smaller. Have you ever looked at a mold plant?

Take a piece of bread and moisten it with water. Leave it out in the air for an hour or so. Then put it into a peanut-butter jar that has some wet paper on the bottom. Screw the top on the jar and put it in some dark, warm place for several days. Soon the mold plants will begin to grow. Watch them each day through your hand lens. The mold will look dark and fuzzy. After it has been growing for a few days, look for little stems with tiny black spore cases on top. The mold plants have taken their food from the bread. They have produced spores that can grow into new mold plants. Pinch one of the black spore cases. What do you find on your fingers?

How does mold spread? To find answers to this question, remember something you did in the previous experiment. You left the bread out in the air before you put it into the jar. Mold spores, then, must be in the air, ready to grow into plants when they find a place where there is food, moisture, and warmth. To see how mold spreads from one food to another, make a mold garden in this way.

Find a moldy orange or lemon. Put it in one of your aluminum-foil pans. Add a few fruits that are not moldy: grapes, a plum, an apple, or a pear — any pieces of fruit will do for this experiment. Arrange them in the pan in a circle around the moldy orange or lemon. Have some

97

of the fresh pieces touch the moldy fruit. Have other pieces several inches away from the mold. Leave your mold garden outside, in a warm place, but where the sun will not reach it. Wait a few days and then watch your mold garden grow.

The mold plants get their food from the fruit on which they are growing, and their moisture from the fruit and from the air. As the mold grows, the spores ripen and are scattered to new areas. The mold spreads first from the moldy fruit to the fresh fruit that is touching it. Little by little, the mold will begin to grow on all the fruit in the pan.

Experiment with different kinds of food in your mold garden. Does mold grow most easily on dry toast or moist bread? Why do people say, "One moldy apple spoils a barrelful?" How many different colors of mold plants can you grow?

Since mold plants take their food from the food in which they grow, you can understand why moldy fruit and bread are not good to eat.

Much of our food is cooked, canned in sealed jars or tins, or frozen in order to keep it from getting moldy. But there are molds that are useful. Some cheeses, for instance, are made from special kinds of mold plants called "cultures" that are added to milk curd. In Roquefort cheese you can see the greenish-black mold. In Swiss cheese the holes are made by gas that is formed while the mold plants grow. The flavors of many different kinds of cheese are caused by the mold plants growing within them.

Perhaps the most wonderful and valuable mold plant in the whole world is the bread mold called "Penicillium notatum." It is from this mold plant that scientists make penicillin, the drug that saves thousands of lives each year.

11

EARTHWORMS

Have you ever noticed earthworms stretched out on the sidewalks after a heavy rain? Do you know why they are there? It is because their underground tunnels have been flooded. As you dig in your garden, you probably find worms in the soil where they live. There are worms all over the world, and many of them are near you most of the time.

There are many different kinds of worms. And there are living things we call worms that are not worms at all. The so-called worms in apples, chestnuts, tomatoes, or ears of corn are insects in one stage of their lives. They look like worms for a while. Then they change into a different stage and don't look like worms any longer. But a real worm does not change its form. It looks and acts the same all of its life.

Earthworms in the soil are true worms. They have no bones. They belong to the largest group of animals in the world, the *invertebrates*, which means animals without backbones.

Earthworms have soft bodies with a nerve running the full length of the underside. They have a circulation system for blood and an amazing digestive tract. They seem to eat anything and everything — meat, cabbage, fruit, leaves, dirt, stones, and even bits of glass. To live, worms must have dirt and small stones. They get food out of the dirt and use the stones to grind it up. Most of the soil that is eaten by a worm passes clear through its body and is discharged as castings. Castings are discharged on the surface of the ground and are valuable in building up rich soil. Earthworms are nature's best plows. They take in the soil, digest it in ways that make the soil rich and fine, and then spread it out as good topsoil. Not only do worms help growing things by making good soil but also by keeping the ground soft and loose so that the rain can soak down to the roots of plants.

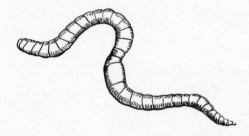

The habits of earthworms are those of burrowing nocturnal (night) animals. They leave their homes in the ground only when they are looking for food, usually at night, or when their tunnels become flooded, or when they are seeking mates. An earthworm crawls backward out of its burrow, feeling around cautiously with its tail. It often keeps its head in its tunnel, ready for a quick escape down the hole. It cannot see or hear. It has to depend on feeling its way.

Worms are extremely dependent on moisture. They

cannot live if their shiny soft bodies become dry. One day in dry air will kill a worm. When the surface of the ground becomes dry, or when it gets very cold or very hot, worms crawl deeper into the soil. In winter they hibernate, often several of them coiling up together in a burrow.

To find out more about earthworms, dig down about twelve inches into your garden soil. Lift the soil out carefully with your spade or shovel and place it in a cardboard carton. Now, using your bare hands, sift through the soil. Make a list like this of the different things you find:

    Earthworms

    Roots of plants

    Ants

    Slugs

    Beetles

    Bits of dead leaves

    Seeds

    Other things

If your soil is the usual kind found in gardens, and if you search carefully, you should find an earthworm or two because they live in the topsoil of most gardens and feed on plant and animal materials in the soil, and on the soil itself. If there are many worms in your garden soil, it is because there is enough moisture and food in loose earth to keep them healthy. If no worms are there, probably the soil is too dry, hard-packed, and lacking in decaying plant and animal material that worms need for food.

You can experiment with an earthworm. Capture a live one and put it on a box top where you can study it with your hand lens. Notice the divisions or segments of its body. Can you find the thick place that is called the egg case?

When the egg case is filled with fertilized eggs, it moves toward the front end of the worm's body. When the eggs are ready to leave the mother worm, the egg case is slipped over the worm's head in such a way that the eggs are dumped out. They are left in the ground where they hatch into baby worms. There are no males or females among earthworms. Each one is both male and female, and every worm has an egg case.

Watch your living specimen move across the box top. Hold it in your hand and feel its soft, moist body. Watch and feel the way it crawls, curls up, and wriggles. The tail is usually the thin, tapering end. The head, with the mouth, is fatter and rounder than the tail. It is an old superstition that if you cut a worm in two, each half will grow into a complete worm. This is not true, of course, so do not try it. This would only kill the worm, not make a new one.

Watch how the worm uses the muscles of its whole body to move from place to place. A worm is well designed for the life it leads. Its round head pushes its way into the soil. The soil goes in the mouth end of its body, then through its whole length, and is finally discharged as worm casts. Thus, it can literally eat its way deep into the earth.

When you have held and examined the worm thorough-ly, put it back on some moist earth where it can improve your garden as it goes on with its natural life.

You can make a worm farm by using a large glass tank or terrarium. If you do not have one, use a fish bowl or a wide-mouthed glass jar, as large a one as you can find. Carefully dig up some topsoil, worms and all, and put it gently into your tank or bowl or jar. Find some extra worms and add them to your worm farm. Be careful not to hurt the soft bodies of the worms with your shovel. See that the soil is kept slightly moist but not wet. Keep your worm farm outside, away from the hot sun. Leave it alone until the worms get used to their new home. Feed your worms with bits of lettuce and some corn meal or

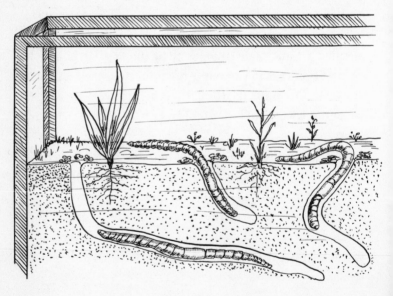

other cereal mixed into the top layer of soil. Add different kinds of leaves, grass, cabbage, etc., from time to time and watch what happens. If your worms make themselves at home in the worm farm, they will soon show it by eating the food and building tunnels in the soil. You may be able to see some of the tunnels through the glass walls of the tank. If nothing seems to be happening after a few weeks, add some more worms and try again. It is possible to start a worm farm in a tank and keep it going for a year or more once the worms have become used to their new home.

Here are some things to remember: Keep your worm farm cool, slightly damp, but never wet, and be sure that there is always some kind of worm food in the soil.

12

SNAILS

Have you ever had the job of spreading "snail bait" among the plants in your yard? If so, you know that snails are regarded as pests because they like to eat fresh green leaves. In this way they sometimes kill young plants and make the leaves and stems of older plants ragged and unhealthy looking. Snails also eat dead and decaying vegetable matter that lies on the ground. When they do this, snails serve as a clean-up squad. They are interesting animals and well worth studying.

The history of snails goes back to prehistoric times when there were many kinds of huge snail-like creatures in the waters of the earth. Today we find fossils of their shells, hundreds of millions of years old. Snails and their relatives still live in water and on land all over the earth.

All snails belong to the mollusk family, a group of invertebrates that have soft bodies. Nearly all of the mollusks protect their soft bodies with hard shells on the outside. These shells grow as their bodies grow. Most mollusks, including many kinds of snails, live in water. Some people like to eat certain kinds of snails. You may not like the idea of eating snails, but you probably do eat clams and oysters, which are also members of the mollusk family.

The snails in your yard could not live in water as some

of the other mollusks do. The common garden snail is a land mollusk and therefore must breathe air. Its scientific name is *Helix hortensis*. It has a soft body, two eyes on tall stalks, a mouth, and one flat, slimy foot. Its shell is spiral, coiled around and around because it grows faster on the outside than on the inside. During the heat of the day, garden snails seek shelter from the sun. They move around at night, gliding slowly over the ground and climbing up and down plants to feed on leaves. In the morning you can trace the shiny trails they have made from the slimy substance that oozes out of the foot of each snail.

Early in the morning collect a few live snails and put them into a glass jar or goldfish bowl. Add a few leaves from the plants the snails have been eating. Place the jar in a shady spot and, with your hand lens ready, wait quietly and see what happens. Can a snail move up the smooth glass wall? Watch the bottom of its foot as it moves. Can you see it expanding and contracting?

As the snail thrusts its soft body out of its shell, notice its head with its two eye-stalks. The moment you touch it, it withdraws into its shell again. Do you see how its

107

shell serves to protect it from birds and other enemies that would use it as food? As long as it lives, a snail cannot leave its shell behind. The foot and the head are pushed out when the snail moves around or when it is eating. But the shell is always there, attached to its body, to serve as a safe hiding place at the first sign of danger.

You can make a permanent snail house from a fish bowl or a glass jar with a cover of wire screening. Put a handful of damp soil on the bottom. Plant two or three flower seedlings or other young plants in the soil. Find six or eight snails of different sizes. Some may be as large around as a quarter. Others may be as tiny as the head of a pin. Put the snails into their new home. Keep them in a cool, shady place and watch them as they begin to move around looking for food. Try adding different kinds of food — bits of lettuce, flower petals, dead insects, some raw hamburg, dry bread, celery leaves. Find out what your snails like to eat and then make sure that there is always enough of it there for them. Keep the soil in the jar moist but not soggy. Keep a record of each snail. If a snail dies, remove it from the jar.

If you had some adult snails to begin with, you may find one day there are some new baby snails in with them. Snails multiply easily, and the babies look exactly like the parents only very, very much smaller. Any grown-up snail can have babies. Like the earthworm, a snail is both male and female. Thus, the mother snail is really the father-mother snail. It is fun to watch the babies eat and grow.

If there are as many snails in your yard as there are in most yards, it will take very little time to make a collection of empty shells. As the snails die, their soft bodies decay rapidly and the hard shells remain behind on the ground. Collect as many shells as you can. Wash them carefully in soapy water, rinse them, and let them dry. Study their patterns and colors. Do you see how they blend with the colors of the soil? This color scheme helps protect snails from their enemies, because the shells are hard to see when they are on the brown and tan soil.

Notice the spiral form of a shell. It grew from the tiny spiral in the center to the large coil on the outside. At the exit of the shell is a beautifully formed rim or lip from which the living snail once pushed its head and foot in and out. The smooth, curved rim, like the graceful edge of a china dish, made it easy for the snail's soft, tender body to slide back and forth without getting hurt.

The shells of garden snails nearly always coil to the right as they grow. Once in a while there is a left-handed shell. If you find one, you will know that you have discovered something rather rare. Arrange your shells in a box or glue them to a piece of heavy cardboard for an exhibit. You might like to arrange them according to color, from darkest to lightest brown; or according to size, from smallest to largest. Or you may want to glue down some good specimens in different positions, showing top, bottom, sides, and openings. If you want to give your collection a scientific label, write this on a card:

MOLLUSK SHELLS — LAND SNAILS
"HELIX HORTENSIS"

As you were looking for good shells for your collection, you may have noticed some broken old shells lying around on the ground. Some of these may have been there for many months or even years. Pick up a few of these old shells. Notice how thin and fragile they are. This is because they have been worn away by rain or snow or the action of wind and sand. Crumble some of the old shells in your hand or pound them with a rock. This is what happens to all snail shells. They are worn away, crumbled, or crushed, and finally they become part of the earth's crust.

13

INSECTS

Lying on your stomach in the grass, you hear the sounds of a teaming world of tiny creatures . . . the small distant siren of the circling fly, the crack-crack of a grasshopper's wings, the buzzing of bees near the flowers, and the faint, faint rustle of insects in the grass. What do you know about the insects that make these summer sounds?

Of all living things in the world, more than half are insects. Insects have no bones and are, of course, invertebrates. Since there are over 500,000 kinds of insects, there are many differences among them. Yet all of them are alike in several important ways.

First, all insects in their adult life have six legs. Second, the adult insect's body always has three parts: head, thorax (the middle part), and abdomen. Third, all insects go through definite changes in form during their lives. These changes are called metamorphoses.

Usually there are four stages in an insect's life. First comes the egg, then the larva (wormlike stage), then the pupa, and finally the adult insect. Adult insects are male and female. They mate, and then the female lays her eggs. The adults die, the eggs hatch into larvae, and so it continues over and over again.

If all of the eggs laid by the millions of insects in the

world would hatch, and if insects did not have so many enemies that use them for food, the earth would be packed full of insects in no time at all. It is a good thing for us that nature has ways of keeping down the insect population. As it is, the total number of insects on the earth is unknown. Scientists think that there are probably about 25,000,000 insects for every square mile of land in the world. That means that we share the earth with billions and billions of insects. Some of them are helpful and some of them are our enemies. All of them are interesting.

How many different kinds of insects live in your yard? First, look for adult insects. They are easier to recognize than insects in any of the baby stages. Look for creatures that have six legs and bodies with three parts (head, thorax, and abdomen). True insects also have two antennae, or feelers. Some have two pairs of wings, some have one pair, and some have no wings at all. Here are some of the insects you may find in your yard:

Ants of different sizes and different colors

Termites — like winged ants. They eat dead wood

Flies of different sizes and different colors

Mosquitoes — members of the fly family

Moths — flying insects with feathery antennae

Butterflies — flying insects with slender, plain antennae with knobs on the ends

Grasshoppers — jumping insects that may spit "tobacco juice," a brown liquid, on you when you catch them

Katydids — something like grasshoppers but harder to see because their wings look like green leaves

Bees — found around flowers and often around a bird bath or other pool or puddle of water

Crickets — shiny black or brown insects with long graceful antennae. Crickets "sing" by rubbing their wings underneath

Beetles — hard-shelled insects of many kinds. The shell is a pair of hard protective wings folded back over a pair of soft flying wings. Beetles form the largest insect group in the world

Lightning bugs or *fireflies* — beetles that make cold, bright lights when they fly at night

Ladybugs — beetles with red-orange shell wings over soft flying wings

June bugs — black, shiny beetles

Dragonflies — with long slim bodies and two pairs of shining transparent wings. They look like small airplanes when they glide

How many of these insects visit or live in your yard? How many other kinds can you find? What kinds of insects are most plentiful where you live? Which kinds do you want to know more about?

Ant   Termite

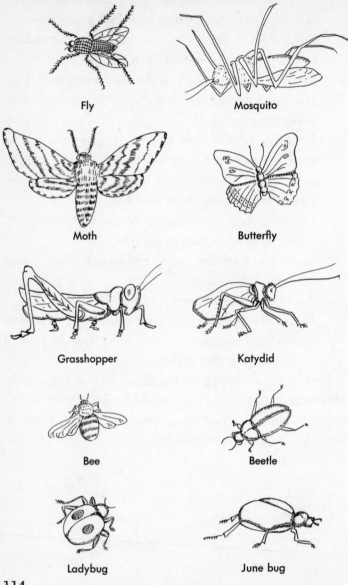

Fly

Mosquito

Moth

Butterfly

Grasshopper

Katydid

Bee

Beetle

Ladybug

June bug

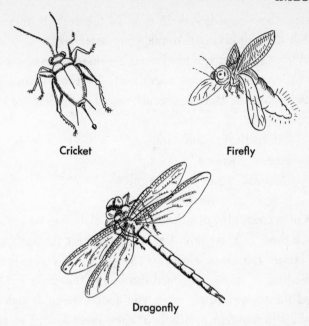

Cricket

Firefly

Dragonfly

You will want to find out what insects are like during each of the four stages of their lives.

Collect the eggs of insects in any of the following ways. Look for small eggs on the undersides of leaves, on tree trunks, or on garden vegetable plants.

Put a piece of spoiled food (potato, tomato, carrot, or other vegetable) on the bottom of a jar. Catch six or eight ordinary flies and put them into the jar. Cover the jar with a circle of wire screen. The female flies in the jar will lay their eggs on the decaying food.

Catch several large grasshoppers and keep them in a screen-covered jar. Put some growing grass in sod on the bottom of the jar. If any of your grasshoppers are fe-

115

males, they may lay their eggs in the sod. If they do, watch the egg-laying through your hand lens.

When an insect egg hatches, it becomes a larva, a small wormlike creature that spends all its time eating and growing bigger. Here are some insect larvae that are easy to find:

Caterpillars, many kinds

Tomato "worms"

"Worms" from wormy apples

Maggots, the larvae of flies

Collect samples of different kinds of living larvae and place them in glass jars. Use a separate jar for each kind of larva. Put some twigs in the jar to give the larvae something to crawl on. Feed the larvae the same kind of food they were eating when you found them. Watch the way the larvae tear or nibble or chew their food. Use your hand lens. Notice how fast they grow.

As you observe your larva specimens from day to day, you will see that they are getting bigger and bigger and less and less active. Then, one day they will stop eating. The larva stage is over. The pupa stage has begun.

Some insects end the larva stage by spinning cocoons. Cocoons are silken cases that some larvae form about their own bodies. There are many different kinds of cocoons. Some are beautiful in color and design. Each of them is a safe, quiet little place where the insect stays until the pupa stage is over. It lives off the fat stored in its body during the larva stage. The pupa seems to be asleep. During this time, great changes are taking place inside and outside its body, getting it ready for the adult stage of insect life. Some pupae stay in their cocoons all winter long. The pupa stage of mosquitoes, on the other hand, lasts only a few days.

Keep any cocoons that have developed from the larvae in your collection. Find others and keep them in cages or jars or boxes with air holes in the top. Write the date you find each cocoon. Keep track of the length of time it takes for each pupa to develop into an adult insect. Leave your cocoons outside even in the cold of winter. The insects that stay in the pupa stage all winter are prepared for cold weather. Then, when warm days arrive in spring, they will be ready to leave their cocoons as adult insects.

Sooner or later, every live insect is ready to break out of its cocoon. Some do this by splitting, tearing, or biting a hole in one end. Others have a liquid in their bodies which softens or dissolves the strands from which the cocoons were made. Make regular observations of your cocoon collection and when you see an insect beginning to break out, watch the process through your hand lens. As soon as a winged insect frees itself from its cocoon, it dries its wings. Then it is ready to fly. When this happens, let the insect go. It will find a mate of its own kind. Then the female will lay many, many eggs, and the main work of its short life will be over.

Some insects die right after mating and laying eggs. Others live through the summer. A few can keep alive during the winter and still live and lay more eggs the

117

next spring. For most insects, however, adult life is a short period indeed.

In each stage of its life history or metamorphosis an insect has certain functions. How many of these have you observed in your study of insects in your yard?

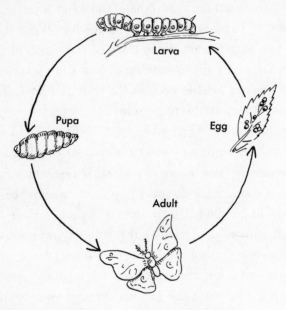

INSECT STAGES	MAIN FUNCTIONS
Egg	To hatch into larva
Larva	To eat and eat, and grow and grow; to spin a cocoon and change into a pupa
Pupa	To remain inactive while nature changes it into an adult

Adult   To break out of the cocoon,
                               mate, lay eggs, and die

You have probably noticed that most insects eat continuously during the larva stage and that some insects eat little or nothing during the other three stages. This is true of many insects. Adult silk moths do not eat at all. There are other moths and butterflies that only sip nectar daintily from flowers during their adult lives. But adult grasshoppers eat voraciously. Great swarms of grasshoppers can lay bare a whole field of grain or strip the leaves from an orchard in a few hours. Crickets, mosquitoes, and other flies also do much feeding during the adult stage.

An interesting experiment may be performed with the so-called "social insects." These are insects that live together in colonies. A colony has several different kinds of workers. Each kind of worker does a special job that helps the whole colony. Bees, wasps, termites, and ants are some of the social insects you may see near your home. The easiest of these for collecting and studying in your yard are the ants. To do this best, you will want to make an ant village of your own.

First, look around in the grass and on the soil in your yard and get acquainted with ants. Take a spoonful of sugar with you, and when you see some ants, scatter a few grains of sugar in their path. Find an anthill. Scatter some sugar on it. Watch the ants through your hand lens. Try the same procedure using fine grass seed, bits of

119

crumbled fried bacon, or a few drops of syrup. Find out what your ants like to eat. Follow some of the ants. Do any of them seem to have regular trails? How do they carry bits of sugar or other food? Are any of the ants carrying anything out of their holes? Are they carrying anything in? How do they keep from bumping into each other as they come and go?

You can discover many things about ants simply by watching them around their anthills. But, if you want to find out what goes on in the ants' homes underground, you must make your own ant village. Here's the way to do it.

Take a quart glass Mason jar with a metal screw top and remove the sealer lid. In place of the sealer, cut two circles of fine window screen just the size of the sealer. Find an anthill and with a large spoon carefully fill the jar about three-fourths full of earth from the anthill. Add as many extra ants as you can find from the same hill. These will probably all be ants from a single colony. You can move ants from the ground to your jar by letting the ants climb onto a small twig and then shaking them off into the jar. Another way is to make a paper funnel and drop the ants in carefully.

Put the circles of screen on the jar as soon as the ants are in it. Otherwise they will climb back out. Sprinkle a few drops of water on top of the soil in your jar and scatter some grass seed and a bit of sugar on the top. A small piece (about one inch square) of plastic sponge that is kept wet will give your ants all the water they need.

Finally, screw the jar ring on over the circles of screen and wrap the glass sides of the jar with a layer of black construction paper.

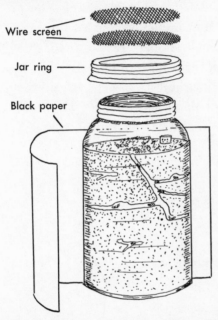

Wire screen

Jar ring

Black paper

The ants now have a new home. They will not be able to climb through the double layer of screen. They have a place to build their underground homes and some food to eat. Leave the paper around the jar. Take it off only when you want to find out what is happening inside the jar. Once the ants feel at home, they will go about their regular lives, building rooms and tunnels. Watch how they carry bits of earth to the surface as they dig, where they store their food, how they keep their homes tidy, and how they clean their own bodies. Try different kinds of

121

food and find out what your ants like best.

From time to time, add a few ants from different ant-hills. What happens to these strangers? How do your ants behave when ants of different size or color are added to the village? How do the newcomers behave?

You will think of other ways of finding out about ants as you watch them for a while each day. Whole books have been written just about ants. If you want to find out what some of the scientists know about life in an ant colony, there are library books that will tell you.

14

SPIDERS

Have you ever walked out into the garden early in the morning and seen a jeweled web glittering with dew, hanging from the bushes? Have you wondered sometimes about the little creature that spun this delicately lovely network of silk? You know, of course, that the web-builder is a spider. How did the spider learn to make such a perfect thing and to suspend it so securely? Why do spiders weave webs? Are they of any use to us?

Of all the animals in your yard, perhaps the most wonderful are the spiders. You may think a spider is a kind of insect, but that is not so. Spiders are invertebrate animals. They have no backbones. Some people think spiders are ugly and dangerous. Perhaps this is why so many people are afraid of them and want to kill every spider they see. It is wrong to kill spiders, because they are among man's most useful friends. Spiders catch and eat flies, mosquitoes, grasshoppers, and other insects that spread disease or destroy fruits, flowers, and vegetables. Without spiders there would soon be so many insect pests around that people would have trouble indeed.

In order to live, raise their babies, and catch the insects they need for food, spiders have special abilities that no other animals possess. All female spiders can spin silk from a liquid made in their bodies. This liquid flows out through four or more spinnerets located at the end of the abdomen. The liquid hardens as soon as it reaches the air. To spin a wide strand of silk, the spider spreads its spinnerets apart. To make a fine strand, the spinnerets are held close together. Some spiders comb the strands together with their hind legs to make solid sheets of silk.

Different kinds of spiders use their silk in different ways. Many build webs, silken traps to catch insects. The trap-door spider spins a silken hinge for the door at the top of its home. Some spider mothers spin silken sacs for their young. Nearly all young spiders spin silk strands into balloons or parachutes that carry them along in the breeze. There are kinds of spiders that never make webs. But even these spiders can spin silk that they use for one purpose or another during some stage of their lives.

The female spider is much larger than the male — larger, busier, and more interesting. It is the female that spins the largest webs, catches the most insects for food, and provides for the young. The male spider spins tiny webs or none at all, catches only a few insects for its own food, and comes around only at mating time. When the mating is over, the female usually traps the male and eats him.

A spider has no real jaw for biting or chewing its food. Its mouth merely sucks in the soft parts of the bodies of insects or other spiders. On each side of a spider's mouth there are two poison fangs, which the spider uses to inject tiny jets of poison into insects that are too powerful to be handled any other way.

Although spiders usually have eight eyes, they cannot see very well. Most of them are near-sighted. They use their sense of touch in many things they do. The short hairs on their legs and bodies help them feel when something is near. Another help is the pair of small "feeler-legs" that grow out of the spider's head. These are not used as legs, but, with the fangs, help the spider to catch and hold its food.

Spiders, even though there are so many of them, do not live in groups or colonies. Every spider looks after itself from an early age. When the baby spiders hatch out of the pearly eggs, which the mother has laid in a silken sac, they get their food in an interesting way. They eat each other! That is, the stronger babies eat up the weaker ones, for spiders are cannibals. When the young spiders are old enough, they drop from their silk cradle and search for tiny insects to eat.

When the time comes for each little spider to go off by itself and find a new home, it climbs to the tip of a tall blade of grass and shoots out strands of silk. A breeze blows the silk and the spider to a higher plant. Then the spider sends forth more strands of silk until the breeze carries it up again. This continues over and over until the little spider is floating along high in the air, above plants and trees, houses and towns. Scientists have found out that young spiders may be carried for hundreds and hundreds of miles in this way, ballooning along in the breeze. Wherever the spider lands, that becomes its home. No wonder, then, that there are spiders all over the face of the earth.

It is interesting to compare a spider with an ant that has no backbone either, but still is an insect. Catch a spider in a small glass bottle. Try not to hurt it. Catch a large ant in another bottle. Examine them both, using your hand lens. You will notice the following:

The ant has six legs; the spider has eight

The ant's body is divided into three parts; the spider's, into two

The ant has long feelers; the spider has fangs, but no feelers

The ant has the three main characteristics of an insect, but the spider has none of these. Spiders belong to a separate class of invertebrate animals, the Arachnida.

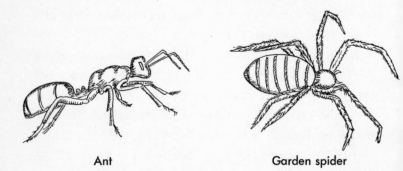

Ant   Garden spider

To find out what different kinds of spiders live around your house and yard, you must organize a spider hunt. Several friends may work together. If you plan to keep the spiders you catch, you will need a jar, with holes punched in the top, for each one. If you put several together in one jar, some of them will probably eat each other.

Do not handle spiders with your bare hands because spiders sometimes bite when they are frightened. Spider bites, except those of the black widow, are usually no more annoying than a mosquito bite, but you can catch spiders without risking any bite at all. Carry a small box with a lid and shake the spider into it. Then put on the lid and carry the spider to the jar where you plan to keep it for observation. Shake it into the jar and go back for another spider. Here are some different kinds of spiders to look for.

Garden spiders. These spiders weave the lacy, round orb webs you sometimes find hanging from bushes and sparkling with early morning dew. Orb webs are hung up and down to catch flying or jumping insects. A garden spider can build a web several feet in diameter in an hour. If the web is torn, the spider generally makes a new web rather than try to repair the old one. If you find a garden spider with its orb web, watch what happens when an insect is caught. Usually the spider will shake the web to make sure that the insect is completely trapped. Then one of several things may happen. If the spider is not hungry, she may weave silk around the insect and thus "keep him in storage" for a future meal. Or she may begin at once to eat the soft parts of the insect's body. If the insect keeps moving around and trying to escape, the spider will put a tiny bit of poison into him through her fangs. This kills the insect, and the spider can have a quiet meal.

Garden spiders are plentiful. You will find their webs off the ground, but not too high to reach. When you find the familiar orb web, the spider may be sitting in the middle of it. Or she may be waiting somewhere at the end of one of the silk guy lines where a pull at the line will let her know that something has been caught in her web.

Triangle spiders. These are named for the shape of their webs. Each web has four main threads fastened together at one end and spread out at the other to make a triangle.

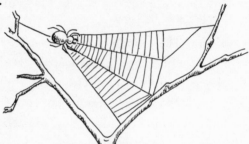

Trap-door spiders. This kind of spider does not make a web. Instead, it digs a hole in the ground, sometimes as much as six inches deep. The hole is lined with a paper-like material made by the spider from a liquid from her own body. This same material is used to make a door at the top of the hole. The hinge is made of silk. The outside of the door is covered with bits of soil and plant material, making it hard to see. The spider sits inside the hole, holding the door shut with its front claws. When an insect wanders by, the spider flings the door open, pounces on the insect, and drags him into the hole.

House spiders. These are the common spiders that build cobwebs. Cobwebs have no special form. Yet they are marvels of construction in their own way, suspended as they are from lamps, ceilings, window frames, and bookcases. Mothers do not like cobwebs because they make a room look untidy. Yet the spiders that spin these webs are catching and eating flies, mosquitoes, and other insects that are dangerous or unpleasant to live with. Cobwebs are better flytraps than any you can buy. If you sweep away a cobweb in the morning, it will usually be rebuilt by night.

Black widows. The black widow is the only spider that is dangerous to man. It is a cobweb builder and sometimes lives indoors, especially in basements, under porches, under logs, or in other dark places near the ground. The female black widow is shiny and black, with a red spot shaped like an hour glass on her underside.

129

She carries a deadly poison which she can inject into her enemies. The bite of a black widow can cause great pain, severe illness, and even death in rare cases to human beings. Fortunately, there are not many black widow spiders around. It is well, however, not to go spider-hunting in dark places and not to handle any spiders with your bare hands.

Grass spiders. These spiders weave an interesting funnel web in the grass. The bottom of the funnel is open. Under it waits the grass spider for some insect to fall into the funnel web. Look for funnel webs early in the morning when the dew on the strands of silk makes them clearly visible in the grass.

Flower spiders or *crab spiders*. These spiders get their names because, like crabs, they can move swiftly backwards and sideways as well as forward, and because they are usually found on flowers. Flower spiders do not build webs. They catch insects that visit their flower homes. A flower spider living within the petals of a white daisy or other white flower will be white. One living in a yellow flower will be yellow.

Tarantula spiders. The tarentulas are the largest of the spider family. They do not make webs. They merely hide and pounce on their insect meals. Tarantulas look hairy, fierce, and dangerous, mainly because they are so much bigger than other spiders. Many other spiders, when viewed through a magnifying glass, look very much like tarantulas. The main difference between tarantulas and other spiders is size.

130

To collect spider webs makes an interesting project. Early some morning in summer or fall, find a fresh orb web. Notice how beautifully it is suspended, with just the right amount of tension to hold the fine delicate, and yet strong strands of silk in shape. Balance and design are perfect. How is a little spider able to create such an engineering masterpiece? No one knows. The first web a spider makes is as perfect as its fifth or tenth or last.

To make and keep a permanent collection of orb webs, you will need to have the following materials:

A small spray-top can of black or white enamel

A sheet of black or white tagboard, map board, or construction paper

A pair of scissors, any kind

A spray-top can of plastic spray. (You will not need this unless you wish to keep your specimens for a permanent collection.)

This is the way to capture a perfect web. When there is no wind, spray the spider web gently with black or white enamel. Spray on both sides. The strands of silk will now be very sticky. If you use black enamel, mount the web on white paper. Use black paper with white enamel. Ease the paper carefully against the web, trying to touch all strands at one time. The web will stick to the paper the moment it touches. Then, with your scissors, cut the guy lines, the strands of silk from which the web is hanging. You now have a complete and perfect web captured on your paper. Lay it flat to dry. To protect it for a permanent collection, spray the entire web on the paper with plastic spray. Label your specimen, ORB WEB FROM GARDEN SPIDER, and add the date. It will be a beautiful thing to frame or to hang on the wall as it is. Spiderweb "pictures" like this may be used for decorations or gifts, or may be kept in a folder as a collection.

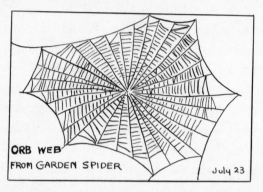

As you study different kinds of webs and become acquainted with the spiders that live in your yard, perhaps you will discover that they are not ugly creatures after all, but marvelously wonderful animals and good friends to man.

15

BIRDS

Have you ever closed your eyes on a quiet summer day and listened to bird sounds? You may have been able to recognize some of the birds around you — the mournful coo of a dove, the early morning song of a robin or a mocking bird, the chirping of sparrows, the soaring trill of a meadow lark, or even the rat-tat-tat of a woodpecker on a telegraph pole.

When you open your eyes and look at the birds, their colors also help you to know them. You see the shining black of a crow, the blue of a blue jay, the orange-red breast of a robin, and the white-striped brown of an English sparrow. Birds are interesting to listen to and interesting to watch. As you explore your yard, you will enjoy finding out about the birds.

Man has always been impressed by the wonders of bird life. There are many puzzling questions about birds, many things that are not known. As you observe the birds around you, you will begin to understand how bird study can be a lifetime hobby for so many people. It would be wonderful indeed to discover the answers to some of the bird mysteries.

How are birds able to fly? How do they take off, soar, swoop, glide, turn, dive, and come in for a landing? What are the mechanics of bird flight? Why do some birds fly thousands and thousands of miles, back and forth from one climate to another? Why do other birds stay in the same area all year long? How do birds know how to build nests? Why do most kinds of birds build new nests every year while a few kinds of birds will return to the same nests year after year? How can birds fly for long distances over desert or sea? Even in New York City there are dozens of different kinds of birds lighting on roof tops, visiting the parks and squares, seeking out food, water, and nesting places. Why do they stay in the city? These are some of the questions that scientists have studied, but they do not know all of the answers.

Do you know what a bird is, scientifically? First of all, a bird is an animal with a backbone. In fact, birds are the most common vertebrates in the world. No matter where you live, you will find birds in your neighborhood. All birds have feathers, two legs, two wings, are warm-blooded and lay eggs. Some birds cannot fly, but they all have wings, whether they use them for flying or not. Any egg-laying animal with feathers, wings, and backbone is a bird.

"She eats like a bird," is a common saying, meant to describe someone who eats very little. Actually, anyone who really "eats like a bird" eats almost all the time and consumes great amounts of food. In an experiment it was discovered that a young robin ate fourteen feet of earthworms in one day.

Birds use up much energy, which food provides. Their

hearts are large in proportion to their bodies, and they have the highest body heat of all animals. A person's normal body temperature is 98.6 degrees. The temperature of an average bird is 110 degrees. We breathe about sixteen times a minute. A bird breathes from one hundred to three hundred times a minute. All of this heat and activity uses up food rapidly. So, for their size, birds need much more food than people do.

Life would be difficult, uncomfortable, or perhaps impossible without birds. Why are birds so valuable to man? The answer lies in the things birds eat.

Different kinds of birds eat different kinds of food. Mostly, they eat things that man wants to get rid of, especially insects, the seeds of weeds, and mice and other small rodents. Even though birds sometimes destroy some of our good fruit and eat some of our good seeds, the small damage that they do is nothing compared with the great value they have in keeping down the population of pests in the world.

Birds have other values, too. Some birds are good to eat, some lay eggs that we use as food, and nearly all birds are beautiful to look at. Then, too, there are the lovely sounds of birds, their songs and chirpings, which add so much to our enjoyment of the outdoors. It is pleasant to live in a world where there are birds.

Watch the birds in your yard and try to find out what foods they are eating. Some are probably eating insects from tree bark. Others are eating the seeds from flower heads, or the ripe fruit on a peach tree, or the nectar of

135

honeysuckle blossoms, or worms from the garden soil. Birds will visit or live in places where they can find the kinds of food they prefer. One way of classifying birds is according to the type of food they eat. Do you have any of the following kinds of birds in your yard?

Seed-eaters. Finches, native sparrows, juncos, grosbeaks, crows, and many others prefer seeds for their diets. Seed-eaters usually have short, thick, strong bills, which are useful for cracking seeds.

Sparrow, a seed-eater

Fruit-eaters. This group includes such common birds as mockingbirds, cedar waxwings, catbirds, thrashers, hermit thrushes, and robins. Their bills are usually longer and more pointed than the seed-cracking bills of the group above.

Insect-eaters. Woodpeckers, flickers, nuthatches, and other birds with long, strong bills like to feed on insects. The blue jay, another insect-eater, also likes nuts and corn.

Nectar- and sap-eaters. Hummingbirds, with their slender bills and their long darting tongues, drink the nectar

Robin, a fruit-eater

Hummingbird, a nectar-eater

Woodpecker, an insect-eater

from flowers. Sapsuckers, with strong bills like those of woodpeckers, drill round holes in tree trunks and then use their bristly tongues to get the sap.

Flesh-eaters. Flesh-eating birds are usually wilder and less common in most parts of the country. Their bills are strong, curved, and sharp for the purpose of tearing flesh from bones. Eagles, hawks, vultures, and owls are some

137

of the meat-eaters. They help to keep down the numbers of bats, mice, rats, and other rodents.

Hawk, a flesh-eater

Many of the birds mentioned above will eat a variety of foods. Some like seeds, berries, worms, and dry bread. What is there in your yard for the birds to eat?

The best way to attract birds and to make certain that there are birds around all year is to make a feeding station for your yard. There are important reasons for doing this. First, there is no better way to learn about birds and their ways than to feed them and watch their behavior as they eat. Second, there are many birds that do not migrate. These are the birds that stay around, summer and winter. During the winter and early spring they have a hard time finding enough food, especially in the city, unless people help them. Third, by attracting birds to your feeding station you will add to the beauty of your neighborhood. If the birds are fed, they will stay in or near your yard, sing, fly, build nests, and raise their young.

The simplest feeding station is any small old table,

shelf, or wooden platform high enough off the ground so that cats and dogs cannot reach it. It may be fastened to a tree, to the side of your house, or mounted on top of a pole. If the platform or feeding tray is placed near a window, you will be able to watch the birds without disturbing them. A low frame or border around the platform will keep the food from being scattered on the ground. It is a good idea to provide some shelter from rain, wind, or snow over at least part of the platform.

Once your feeding station is in place, experiment with different kinds of food and watch what your birds prefer. Below is a list of foods recommended by the U. S. Fish and Wildlife Service for winter feeding of common birds.

KIND OF BIRD	FAVORITE FOODS
Titmouse, chickadee, nuthatch	Suet, cracked nuts, broken peanuts, sunflower seeds, bread crumbs
Mockingbird, catbird, thrasher, hermit thrush, robin	Cut apples, cut oranges, currants, raisins, bread crumbs
Blackbird, cardinal, towhee	Sunflower seeds, corn, broken peanuts, scratch feed
Finch, junco, native sparrow	Scratch feed, millet, wheat screenings, small seed mixtures, bread crumbs

139

Woodpeckers   Suet, cracked nuts, corn

Birds will also eat many kinds of table scraps. Try a variety and see what happens. Which birds pick out the fruit? Which birds prefer suet and bits of meat? Which ones seem to eat anything they can get?

There is another way in which you can attract birds to your yard. Birds like to bathe, especially in hot, dry weather. Even when the air is chilly, many birds like to splash in water. Any simple bird bath will attract birds. They will fly in for a bath and a drink. Like the feeding station, the bath should be off the ground, out of reach of cats and other animals. Any shallow tray that will hold water may be mounted on a post or placed on top of a tree stump. An easy way to make a birdbath is to use an old hub cap from an automobile wheel. Put the hub cap on top of a post. Put in some sand or gravel to provide a safe foothold, fill with water, wait a while, and then watch the fun. Early in the morning is a favorite bathing time

for many birds. Once the birds have found their new bathing place in your yard, they will come back day after day. Be sure to keep the bath clean and filled with water at all times.

Anyone, in the city or in the country, can be a bird watcher, and you may want to be one, too. The important thing is to know what to look for while you are watching. Here are some things to notice when you do your first bird watching.

Is the bird alone, with one other bird, or in a flock?

What is the bird's main color?

What are the special markings, if any? (White lines on wings, red throat, orange breast, etc.?)

About how big is the bird? Compare it with birds you know: smaller than a sparrow, as big as a robin, almost as big as a pigeon, etc.

Does the bird hop, run, or walk?

What kinds of sounds does it make? Does it chirp, trill, caw, chatter, repeat a definite sound pattern?

What kind of bill does it have? Is it short and thick for seed-cracking? Is it long and thin to pick insects from cracks? Is it sharp and curved to tear meat?

What kind of food is the bird looking for?

What is the shape of the bird's tail?

Does it have long or short legs, and are its feet large or small?

Answer these questions for every kind of bird you watch. Add other facts you notice. If you keep a bird diary with dates and places and descriptions of birds you see, you will soon have a valuable record of the birds in your neighborhood. Audubon Bird Cards, from the National Audubon Society, 1000 Fifth Avenue, New York 28, New York, will help you to identify and learn the names of the birds you watch.

Once you have learned to study birds by watching them with your own two eyes, you may want to try using a pair of opera glasses or a pair of binoculars, which are more powerful magnifiers. Then you can see many details you had not noticed before.

It is best to watch birds very early in the morning. Get up about four o'clock and go quietly outside. Stand with the rising sun at your back. Wait, listen, and watch. This is the time of day when birds are most "watchable." Do not make any sudden motions. Just watch quietly, and when you move, move slowly. Make written notes about the birds you see and hear.

When you have had some practice in bird watching in your own yard, you may want to organize an early morning bird-watching trip to a park, field, or the edge of a woods. Or you may be able to join a bird-watching group already organized in your community. Most towns have bird watchers. The grownups in these groups are usually happy to welcome a young person who is truly interested in bird life and who knows how to watch quietly.

It is interesting to make a collection of birds' nests. Most birds desert their nests as soon as the baby birds have flown away. A nest is built for only one purpose, to raise the young. Hence an empty, deserted nest has no

142

further use and may be removed for your collection. Late fall and winter are especially good times for collecting birds' nests. By then, with most of the leaves off trees, bushes, and vines, the nests can be seen easily.

Different kinds of birds build different kinds of nests. Nests are usually placed where they will be protected from strong winds, heavy rains, direct sunlight, and from enemies. Keep a record of the various places you find nests. Some may be in tall grasses on the ground, some in weeds and bushes, some in the lower branches of trees, some under the eaves of your house, and some in hollow trees. There are some that you will not see at all, for they are at the tops of tall trees.

When you find a nest, make a note of the exact place you found it. Was it built —

in the fork of a tree limb?

among some climbing vines?

in a hollow tree?

hanging from the tips of long branches?

under the eaves of a house or other building?

in a man-made bird house?

some other place?

Nesting places, as well as types of nests, help bird scientists identify the builders of the nests. The Baltimore oriole, for instance, hangs its beautifully made bag-shaped nest from the tips of branches. The goldfinch builds a firm cuplike nest on solid branches. Barn swallows attach their bracket nests to a wooden beam. Other birds have their own style of nest-building. Some people

143

learn to identify birds by first learning to recognize the kinds of nests they build.

Birds build their nests of the materials around them. Find out what the different birds in your neighborhood are using as building materials. To do this, place one of the nests in your collection on top of a clean piece of paper. Have several glass jars, tin cans, or cardboard boxes within easy reach. Then, most carefully, bit by bit, take the nest apart. Put all the material of one kind into one box or jar. Use a different jar for each kind of material until the entire nest has been taken apart. Make a list of all the things used by the bird in making this paricular nest.

Did you find any twigs? How many?

Any bits of dry leaves? How many?

Any animal hair? How many strands?

Any fibers from dandelions or milkweeds? How many?

Any bird feathers or down? How many bits?

Any strands of moss or lichens? How many?

Any flower petals? How many?

Any other bits of natural materials? How many?

Any bits of "man materials": cotton, string, paper, rags, shavings, tinfoil, yarn, etc.? How many?

Anything else? How many bits?

How many *separate bits* of building materials did this bird use? Next, count the different *kinds* of nest-building materials you found in this one nest. Then think about the following questions.

Where did the bird get the materials for this nest?
How many separate flights do you think she made to
gather these bits of materials?
What kind of material was most used in this nest?
Can you figure out why?
Now that you have taken apart a bird's nest, do you
think you can put it together again? Try it. Make
the best nest you can make. Then compare it with a
nest made by a bird. Which is a better builder of
nests, you or the bird?

Anyone who spends much time outdoors is certain to
find a dead bird sooner or later. Instead of making a
coffin for it and having a funeral service, why not use it
for some scientific investigations? Why not study its
feathers?

You will find at least two main kinds of feathers. The
large feathers are sometimes called contour feathers or
flight feathers. They help form the bird's shape and also
help in flying. Examine a single large feather from any
kind of bird. If you do not have a dead bird handy, use a
contour feather from a chicken, duck, or other domestic
fowl.

Spray the feather with a few drops of water. The water
runs off easily because of an oily coating that causes contour feathers to shed water. The stem of the feather, where
it sticks into the bird, is called a quill. The quill is hollow. This helps to make the bird light so that flight is
easier. You will find the feather flexible, and also tough
and strong. Examine it through your hand lens. Can you

145

see the tiny hooks that hold the edges of the feather together? Contour feathers form the main outer coat.

After you have studied several samples of contour feathers, look for the other main kind, the fluff or down feathers. Examine them through your magnifying lens. Touch them with your fingers. Down feathers form the soft inner coat that holds warm air close to the bird's body.

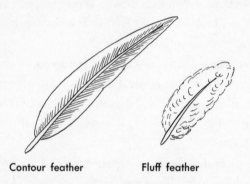

Contour feather   Fluff feather

You can learn other interesting things by studying the bones of birds. An easy way to do this is to save all the bones from a chicken dinner. Scrape off as much of the meat as possible and then boil the bones in soapy water for several hours. Rinse them in clear hot water and place them on newspapers in the sun to dry. The bones should now be clean and white. Notice the following things about bird bones.

Leg bones are hollow. This makes them lighter and stronger than solid bones. Breast bones are large in relation to the other bones in a bird's body. The breast bone is the place to which the bird's strong flight muscles are attached. People do not have large breast bones because they have no flight muscles. Compared with bones from beef (cattle), pork (pigs), mutton (sheep), and other animals we eat, chicken bones are light in weight. A light but strong skeleton helps birds to fly.

The bones of a bird, like its high temperature, rapid heart beat, and special feathers, are perfectly designed for the activities of bird life. All of these things together make it possible for a bird to do the thing man has marveled at most, to rise from the earth under its own power and to soar high into the air.

16

OTHER VERTEBRATE ANIMALS

When you pat your dog or stroke your cat, you can easily feel the backbone that runs the full length of its body. Backbones are called vertebrae. Feel your own backbone. You are a vertebrate animal. So are dogs, cats, and other animals you are familiar with. Birds, as you already know, are the most common vertebrates. But there are many other animals with backbones. Your yard, even if it is a small one and right in the middle of the city, may be the home of other animals of the vertebrate family.

Explore your yard and keep a record of all of the vertebrates that live there or that visit your yard from time to time. Do you ever see any of the following animals in your yard?

Rabbits
Toads
Lizards
Turtles
Snakes
Mice
Gophers
Squirrels

How different snakes are from rabbits, and squirrels from toads! Yet all of them have backbones and so belong to the vertebrate group.

Can you discover any other kinds of vertebrates in your neighborhood? Do some live there all year long? Do some just pass through as they hunt for food and water? If you watch them carefully, you can learn a great deal about their activities. As you observe the differences among them, you will not be surprised to learn that vertebrate animals are divided into several main groups according to their way of living and the structure of their bodies.

It is interesting to study the different groups. To find out about the habits of the fish family, you may want to make an outdoor pond or a glass aquarium. There are many ways of building a little pool in your garden. A shallow hole dug in the ground, lined with concrete and bordered with rocks, will make an ornamental fish pond. Or an old metal washtub or other solid container sunk into the earth and partly filled with clean white sand can become a pool.

An easier way of making a home for fish is to use a regular straight-sided aquarium, a round bowl, a large pickle jar, or any other large-mouthed glass container. Spread clean sand on the bottom and then put in some water plants. They will add to the beauty of your aquarium or pond and also provide food and oxygen for the fish. You may find some water plants growing in streams or ponds. If not, you can buy some for a few cents at a dime store or pet shop.

Goldfish are the easiest kind of fish to care for. They will live outdoors in all but the coldest weather and can be kept indoors in tanks or bowls for months or years.

149

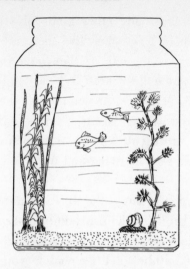

A few water snails will help keep the water clean, as the snails eat the old food and refuse of the fish.

As you watch your fish, you will notice some important things. Fish can live only in water. They breathe through their mouths, and, instead of lungs, fish have gills that take the oxygen from the water. Notice how a fish uses its fins in swimming. The shape of its body helps it to move through the water.

All fish are cold blooded-animals. This means that when the animal is in cold water, its body becomes cold. In warm water, its body heats up. With warm-blooded animals like us, body heat usually stays about the same whether the surroundings are warm or cool.

Most fish will eat insects, insect eggs and larvae, under-water plants, and other fish. If you make an aquarium, you must be careful about putting different kinds of fish

150

together. Some of them may eat the others. The person who sells you your fish will advise you about the kinds of fish that will live safely together. Fish in general are not very intelligent animals, but they are graceful and lovely to watch and as pets are easy to care for.

Another interesting group of vertebrate animals is the amphibians. Toads and frogs are amphibians. Amphibian means literally "living in two places." The name describes the most important difference between this group and all other groups of vertebrates. Amphibians hatch from eggs that have been deposited in ponds or streams and then live in water like fish during the early stages of their lives. They get oxygen from the water by means of gills. Gradually the little fishlike creatures grow lungs and legs and move to land. After that, they have to breathe air.

To watch the development of amphibians, catch some pollywogs in a pond or stream and keep them in water in an aquarium or open jar until they turn into little toads or frogs. Feed them bits of lettuce, dry bread, and tiny insects. Keep a record of how long it takes for a pollywog to turn into an adult, land-living amphibian. The adult amphibians eat different foods than the young. Watch a toad and see how it captures and eats a live fly. Since toads eat flies and other insects, you can see how valuable these amphibians are to man.

If you look carefully at a toad, you will find that it has some interesting features. If you can catch a toad, hold it gently in your hands. Feel its heart beating. Look at its

151

head and its eyes and its mouth and its bumpy skin. People once believed that anyone who touched a toad would get warts. This is just a superstition, for a toad cannot hurt you in any way. Toads are good friends to have in your yard.

Toad

Amphibians are interesting to scientists because they show the link between water-breathing fish and air-breathing reptiles.

You will want to discover what reptiles are in your yard. Sometimes, on a summer day, you may see the tall grass move as the slender body of a snake slithers along the ground. Or you may see lizards sunning themselves on some warm stones. Perhaps you own a pet turtle that lives in a terrarium where it can swim in a little pool of water or climb onto some rocks. These animals all belong to the same vertebrate family. They are reptiles.

Reptiles differ from other vertebrates in several ways. Like fish, they are cold-blooded. Their bodies are usually covered with protective layers of scales or scalelike shells.

152

But, unlike fish and unlike other amphibians, reptiles are air-breathers all their lives. Even those that live in water have to come to the surface for air.

Reptiles lay eggs. When the baby animals hatch, they are usually able, from the very beginning, to take care of themselves. Most reptiles eat great numbers of insect pests. Some of the larger snakes also feed on rats, mice, and other destructive rodents.

Most reptiles can be kept in a cage but must be given special food and care. Since they are cold-blooded animals and cannot adjust their body temperature, they must be protected from extremes of both heat and cold. If you keep a reptile in a cage for observation, be sure to keep it supplied with living insects (flies will usually do), a pan of water for drinking or bathing, and a pile of rocks or some tree branches for climbing.

It is best to keep most reptiles in captivity for only a few days. Often they will not eat in a strange place, so if kept too long they will die. Better than risking the life of one of these friendly animals, turn it loose where you found it as soon as you have had a chance to observe it thoroughly at close range. The following reptiles are common in most parts of the country. How many can you find?

Lizards. Various sizes, shapes, and colors, found in many areas and many climates.

Snakes. Grass snakes, ribbon snakes, garter snakes, gopher snakes, king snakes. All of these are helpful to man. Their bodies, whether long or short, thick

153

or thin, are all gracefully tapering from head to tail. *BEWARE* of snakes with flat triangular or arrow-shaped heads, with diamond markings on their bodies, or with buttons or rattles on their tails. Poisonous snakes have these characteristics. Do not pick up *any* snake unless you are certain that it is one of the non-poisonous kind. Snakes should not be handled until you have learned a great deal about the different kinds that live in your area.

Horned toads. Really horned lizards since they are reptiles and not amphibians. Hot, dry places, especially on deserts, are where these shy, gentle creatures live.

Turtles and tortoises. Found swimming in the water, or walking on land. Of all the reptiles, turtles and tortoises probably make the best pets. They are gentle, easy to handle, and not so delicate as many other reptiles.

Most people agree that mammals are the most important animals in the world. Certainly this is true as far as we are concerned, for we are mammals. Whether mammals are important or not, we do form a group of vertebrates with some very special characteristics and abilities. As you observe the different mammals you have around you, notice that all of them have these four mammal features, regardless of how different they look and how differently they live.

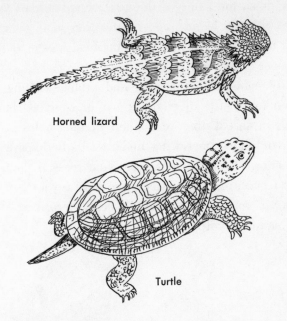

Horned lizard

Turtle

All mammals —

give birth to live babies

feed their babies with milk from their mother's bodies

have four legs (or two arms and two legs)

have hair or fur all over their bodies

You may want to make a book of the mammals you see in your neighborhood, with a separate page for each mammal. You can draw a picture or cut one from a magazine for each page. Here are some suggestions for dividing your book into sections.

Domestic mammals. In this part you will keep notes about dogs, cats, horses, cows, goats, pigs, and sheep.

155

Write down the name of the kind of animal, when and where you see it, and any information you can gather about its fur or hair, its babies, the food it eats, and anything else of interest.

Wild mammals. You may find rabbits visiting your garden for a taste of fresh lettuce, or squirrels hunting acorns in an oak tree, or gophers digging holes in your lawn, or moles burrowing underneath. Perhaps a deer comes down from the hills to eat your roses or the tender green leaves from young trees. Are there any mice or chipmunks in your neighborhood? Keep a record of all the wild mammals you see.

Squirrel

Zoo mammals. If you live near a zoo, you can fill many pages of your book with observations of bears, lions, tigers, elephants, and a host of other animals. Studying zoo animals is a good thing to do if you are especially interested in knowing about all kinds of mammals, or if you cannot find many mammals in your own yard.

Human mammals. There are so many scientific things

to study about people that you could spend your whole life on just this section. You may want to make a special study of yourself, since you are the mammal you know best. Begin with a picture and a description of yourself, the color of your eyes, hair, and skin. Keep a record of your height and weight, the number of hours you sleep, what you eat and drink, and the special things you can do best. If you make such a record, write a date for each entry. Answer the question, "What am I like today, June 25, 19....?" A record of yourself is easy and interesting to make. Such a record, if kept regularly over a period of time, could have scientific value in years to come. There are many scientific discoveries that have been made by people who used themselves for observation and study.

There are science specialists who study all the different things about human beings. It is important to know man's history, how human bodies function, and the ways men have learned to live together in families, communities, and nations. Most marvelous of all is to learn about human intelligence. No other animals in the world are nearly as intelligent as human beings. People can *think*. This makes it possible for us to do many things that no other living creatures have ever been able to do.

17

CLOUDS

Have you ever had the delightful experience of lying on your back on a lazy summer afternoon, just looking up into the deep blue sky and watching fluffy white clouds change from one shape to another? One may have looked like a Colonial gentleman with a cocked hat. In a few minutes, as the clouds billowed up and out, they may have looked like a ship in full sail, and then changed to a crouching lion or a castle on a mountain. If you have watched such a moving-picture show in the sky, you have probably wondered what clouds really are. Have you ever been close to a cloud? Have you ever touched one? Chances are that you have, many times, even though you may not have realized it at the time.

If you've flown in an airplane, you've probably had the exciting experience of flying through clouds and above them. As you passed through the clouds, did you notice what they looked like as they pressed against the window of your plane? They seemed like soft, foggy mist. When you flew above the clouds and looked down on them, you may have discovered that they looked like fluffy white blankets spread out between you and the earth below.

Perhaps you have climbed a mountain, high enough to walk right through a small cloud, and then, from the top of the trail, have looked down on the cloud from above.

Even if you have never traveled in a plane or climbed a cloud-topped mountain, you have probably been in clouds many times. In most parts of the country there are times when clouds come right down to earth and lie on the ground. When a cloud is on the ground, we call it fog. Think of the foggy days you have known. Many of the clouds you see in the sky are just like fog, only higher up. Clouds are made of water vapor and tiny particles of water or ice.

Nearly all of the earth's clouds are in the troposphere, the layer of atmosphere nearest the earth. This is the part of the atmosphere where weather is made. Clouds have a great deal to do with the kind of weather we have.

Watch the sky every day and see how many kinds of clouds you can discover.

All of the clouds listed appear in the bottom (troposphere) layer of the atmosphere. In the atmosphere layers above the troposphere, only two kinds of clouds are known to occur. These rare clouds are called *nacreous* (like mother-of-pearl) and *noctilucent* (glowing at night). They are in the stratosphere and beyond.

Keep a record of the kinds of clouds you see each day. In a notebook or on a chart, write the names of the clouds and a description of the weather of that day. If you keep your record carefully, you will soon discover some relationship between cloud types and weather conditions of the same day and of the day following.

159

CLOUD CHART

Cloud	Description	Found	Weather
Cumulus	White, puffy, like heaps of cotton. The kind of billowing clouds that seem to form pictures. Some tower to 10,000-12,000 feet into the air.	Floating about in the lower atmosphere. May occur any time of year, but seen most often in spring and summer.	Fair, bright, sunny.
Cirrus	Thin, white, wispy curls against bright blue sky. Formed by ice crystals. Move as fast as 200 miles per hour. The highest and fastest clouds.	Always high in atmosphere, sometimes more than 25,000 feet up. May occur any time of year.	Clear, but rain or snow may be on the way.
Stratus	Layers, thin, grayish-white, covering most of the sky. Flat streaks across sky, or misty gray layers on ground.	Near or on the surface of the earth. When lying on the ground, are called fog.	Mist or quiet drizzle; never violent rain.

Nimbus	Long, flat clouds with ragged edges. Dark gray.	Covering a large area of sky.	Rain or snow.
Cumulo-nimbus (Thunderheads)	Towering heaps of white cumulus clouds turning first to light gray, then to darker and darker gray. Flat on bottom, often in form of an anvil.	Most often in summer. May appear in late afternoon or evening of a very hot day.	Electrical storms: thunder, lightning, rain.
Nimbo-stratus	A heavy layer of thick, dark gray clouds.	Covering entire sky at any time of year.	Rain or snow.
Cirro-cumulus	Small, fluffy white clouds. When they occur in even rows like scales of a fish, the pattern is called a mackerel sky.	Fairly high, against a blue sky.	Clear; but rain or snow may be on the way.

Cumulus

Cumulo-nimbus

Cirrus

Nimbo-stratus

Stratus

Cirro-cumulus

Nimbus

KINDS OF CLOUDS

If you are interested in drawing, it is easy to collect cloud samples on paper. Once you are familiar with the different types of clouds, make pictures of them, using white and gray chalk on sheets of blue and gray paper.

> Which kinds of clouds would you make with white chalk on sky-blue paper?
> Which kinds of clouds would you make with light gray chalk on gray paper?
> Which kinds of clouds would you make with dark gray or almost black chalk on gray paper?

Another way of collecting cloud samples is to cut pictures from magazines and newspapers. Paste the pictures in a scrapbook and, if you are a cloud watcher, keep a record of when and where you see real clouds of the same types.

A third way to collect clouds is to take your own photographs of them. Photographing interesting skies is an art as well as a science. Collecting your own cloud snapshots could become a valuable and interesting hobby.

18

WEATHER

As you go outdoors every day, you cannot help noticing differences in weather. Many of the things you do are affected by it. Have you ever found it hard to plan ahead because a change of weather would mean a change in your plans? Have you ever wondered if a day will be —

warm enough for a swim?

snowy enough to go coasting?

cold enough for ice-skating?

too damp for a picnic?

windy enough to fly a kite?

too dry for a bonfire?

too hot for a hike?

calm enough for canoeing?

When you want to know what kind of weather is heading your way, you probably do as most of us do, find out what the weatherman has to say. His report is in the daily newspapers and is broadcast on the radio and on television. Many jokes are made about the times the weatherman's predictions do not come true. But, if you keep a daily record of what the weatherman says and what the weather turns out to be, you will probably find that most of the time the weatherman is right. How does he figure it out?

Clouds help, of course, but there are other conditions in the atmosphere that also make the weather. The weatherman is a scientist, a meteorologist, trained to find out what the different conditions are and how they will affect the weather to come. To do this, he uses special instruments in a weather station.

You can make and use a weather station of your own. In your weather station you will need instruments that will help you keep track of the same atmospheric conditions that are studied by the weatherman. Here are suggestions for collecting or making simple indicators for temperature, air pressure, humidity, precipitation, wind direction, and wind speed.

Temperature. Use an ordinary house thermometer. Hang it outdoors in a shady spot. An ideal place is on a post three to five feet above the ground. Your daily temperature recordings should be made in the shade. If you want to compare shade and sun temperatures, place a second thermometer in a sunny spot.

Air pressure. Take a piece of rubber from a broken balloon. Stretch it over the top of an empty, dry milk bottle. Fasten it tightly with rubber bands. Spread a strip of glue from the center of the rubber to the edge. Place the end of a paper drinking straw horizontally on the glue. Hold it on firmly until the glue dries. Now place the milk bottle against a piece of cardboard from a paper carton. With a black crayon, put a mark on the cardboard exactly level with the end of the straw. When the air pressure becomes greater, the rubber on the top of the

165

bottle will be pushed down and the pointer end of the straw will move up. When the air pressure gets less, the rubber will loosen up and the pointer will move down. Thus when the marks on the cardboard are higher, the pressure is greater (low barometer reading); and when the marks are lower, the pressure is less (high barometer reading). Mark the top of the cardboard "LOW" and the bottom "HIGH." Label the entire scale, "Air Pressure Indicator." This is a simple and not-too-exact barometer. But it will, if made right, show when there is a change in air pressure. You may know someone who owns a mercury barometer or an aneroid barometer. If so, you can perhaps find out what these barometers indicate and compare their readings with those of your homemade barometer.

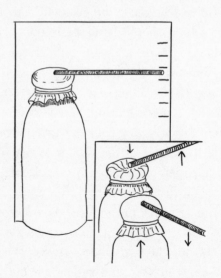

Humidity. To measure the amount of humidity in the air, you will need to make a wet-bulb thermometer. Use a medical thermometer or a regular house thermometer. If the thermometer you use has a little metal cage around the bulb at the bottom, remove the metal so that the bulb is exposed. Then roll a piece of wet cotton cloth around the bulb and let the end of the cloth hang down into a can of water. The cloth will act as a wick. Keep some water in the can at all times and place the wet-bulb thermometer, can and all, near your regular dry-bulb thermometer. Keep a record of dry-bulb and wet-bulb temperatures. There is usually a difference in the two readings.

As you may remember, when water evaporates, heat is used up. Thus, anything next to evaporating water becomes cooler. The water in the cloth wrapping around your wet-bulb thermometer will keep on evaporating as long as the air can hold more water vapor. Dry air can take on more water vapor than air that is already filled with moisture. Thus:

1. *dry air* (low humidity) causes
2. *fast evaporation*, which causes
3. *heat to be taken from bulb*, which causes
4. *lowered temperature reading*, which results in
5. *difference between regular dry-bulb temperature and wet-bulb temperature.*

Considering the first and last steps, the drier the air (that is, the lower the humidity), the greater will be the difference in the two temperature readings. And when the

167

humidity is higher, there will be less difference in the dry-bulb and wet-bulb temperatures. If the two temperatures are ever exactly the same, you will know that the humidity is 100 per cent. That means that the air around you is already filled, or saturated, with moisture. It has all the water vapor that it can hold.

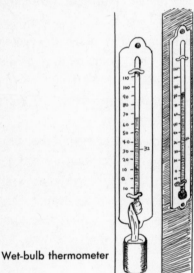

Wet-bulb thermometer   Dry-bulb thermometer

Precipitation. To measure the amount of **water that** falls during a rain, you will need a rain gauge. You can make one from any straight-sided, flat-bottomed glass jar. A peanut-butter or mayonnaise jar will do. Put it in a flat, level open place. Each time it rains, measure the inches and fractions of inches of water in the bottom of the jar. To do this accurately, make a mark on the outside of the jar with a marking pencil or a piece of soap at exactly

168

the level of the water. Then empty the jar, and, with your ruler on the inside of the jar, measure the distance from the bottom of the jar to the mark. Then, for your weather record, write down the date and the exact amount of rain.

You may also want to keep a record of the kind of rain, from your own observation. Was it a heavy, pelting rain? A slow, steady drizzle? Rain and hail? An all-night downpour? Or the kind weathermen call "intermittent showers"? Watch the different kinds of rains and storms and learn to describe them.

Wind direction. To find out where the wind is coming from, you will need to make an old-fashioned weather vane and fasten it to the top of a post or mount it on top of your garage or house. The simplest kind can be cut from heavy corrugated cardboard from a grocery carton. Make it about a foot long and shape it, of course, like an arrow with the widest part at the end opposite the arrow point. Then hold the arrow with the flat side of the cardboard facing you and run a long thin nail vertically through the shaft of the arrow. The openings in the corrugated layer in the cardboard will provide a hole for the nail. Use a small wooden spool for a washer. Run the nail through this and finally hammer the nail into the post or pole on which it is to be mounted. You may have to experiment with different nails and washers before your vane is mounted securely and yet free enough to turn easily with the wind. This cardboard vane will serve for a while, but eventually you may want to carve a permanent one from wood. If so, look first at the weather vanes sold in stores and get ideas for ways of fastening one to a post so that it can turn freely.

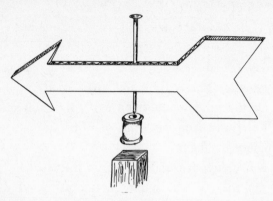

To make use of your weather vane, you will need a compass. First, note the direction the weather vane arrow is pointing. Then, locate that direction on your compass. The wind is coming from that direction. If the arrow points south-east, there is a south-east wind. If the arrow points west, there is a west wind. Keep a daily record of the direction from which the wind is blowing. This will always be the direction in which your weather vane is pointing.

The wind direction will give you a hint about the kind of weather that is on the way. In general, winds carry weather from one place to another. A wind blowing off the North Pole, for instance, naturally is a cold wind and cools off the land it blows over. A wind coming from a hot desert will bring dry heat, and an ocean breeze will bring cool, moist air. Where you live, of course, has a lot to do with the meaning of each kind of wind.

170

Wind speed. A simple anemometer to indicate the speed or velocity of the wind can be made. It will not measure exactly how many miles an hour the wind is blowing, but it will give you a chance to observe differences in wind speed. Make a cross of two thin sticks of wood. Carve each one out in the middle, enough so that the two sticks fit together and make a flat cross. Staple, tack, or wire four small metal-foil pans to the four ends of the cross. The pans in which small pies or tarts are sold are just right. Then, with a fine drill, or with a sharp, thin nail, make a small hole part-way through the center of the cross. This hole should be slightly larger than the head of a pin. Next, stick a strong pin into the eraser on the top of a pencil. Fit the pointed end of the pencil into the hole of a large spool (it should fit snugly) and wire the spool to a brick, a flat stone, or a block of wood. Place this heavy base on a box, on top of a fence or on some solid place about three feet above the ground. Finally, put the wooden cross with the metal foil cups on top of the pin. The hole in the cross should fit over the head of the pin. Blow on the cups. If the cross turns easily, your anemometer is ready. If it sticks or moves in jerks, make the hole in the crossed sticks larger. Sometimes soap or candle wax rubbed over the head of the pin helps the anemometer to turn more easily. Once your instrument is ready to turn as the wind blows, you can begin keeping a record of wind speed.

First, just notice differences in speed from hour to hour and day to day. Sometimes your anemometer may be whirling around very fast. At other times it may be scarcely moving. To measure these differences, paint a colored mark on one of the metal foil pans. Using a watch or an alarm clock, count the number of times the anemometer turns in one minute. Just count the number of times the colored mark moves around to you. Then you can keep your record of wind velocity in terms of "RPM," which stands for number of revolutions per minute. The greater the RPM, the greater the wind velocity.

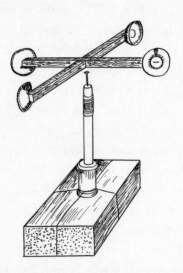

With the instruments described above, you can learn about the changes in the atmosphere around you. You can, using your own hands and your own senses, learn some of the beginning things about the science of meteorology.

It is fun to build, to observe, and to experiment. But,

if you want to be scientific, you will also have to work out ways of keeping a systematic record of what you find. A large sheet of paper, ruled in columns or squares, can be used as a day-by-day weather chart. If you would rather keep a weather notebook, you can make a weather diary. If so, you may add drawings, weather reports cut from the daily newspapers, weather news items, and weather pictures from magazines. Whatever form you choose for keeping track of the findings from your back-yard weather station, there are certain things you will want to note every day. A complete daily record might be something like this:

DATE — July 23

SKY — sunny, with cumulus clouds

TEMPERATURE — 75° in shade; 85° in sun

AIR PRESSURE — Rising; higher than yesterday

HUMIDITY — Rising

PRECIPITATION — None

WIND DIRECTION — S.W.

WIND VELOCITY — Gentle breeze; about 10 RPM

FORECAST FOR TOMORROW — (What would *you* predict?)

If you make a prediction, compare your forecast with that made by the weatherman. Then compare them both with the actual weather as it occurs. Find out some of the reasons why, with all the scientific instruments and trained specialists on the job, weather predictions do not always come true.

19

ATMOSPHERE AND OUTER SPACE

When the air is clear and you look straight up (that is, away from the surface of the earth), you can look right through the miles and miles of atmosphere and see the moon, planets, and stars far off in outer space. You are probably so accustomed to living in the atmosphere, breathing it and looking through it that you may never have thought much about it. Think about it then, for a few moments.

What do you *see* as you look into the atmosphere? Is the air clear and blue, fog-gray, smog-brown, colorless, or pink and gold from the setting sun?

What do you *feel?* Is there a wind or a breeze? Is the air hot, dry, cold, or moist? Is there any precipitation, like rain, snow, or hail?

What do you *hear?* Is the air quiet or filled with sounds? Can you hear rain or the rumble of thunder?

What do you *smell* and *taste?* Is there sand or dust in the air, or salt spray from the sea, or smoke from factories, or wood smoke from a fireplace or campfire, or gasoline fumes from city streets?

As you explore the atmosphere with your five senses, you are really exploring only the very bottom of hundreds of miles of atmosphere layers that wrap the earth. The layer in which you live has oxygen for breathing, and enough air pressure, moisture, and all the other atmospheric conditions that make life possible.

Whenever we speak of layers of anything, we are likely to picture a sandwich or a layer cake, with neat, separate layers. But there are no exact dividing lines between the different layers of atmosphere. Each one blends gradually into the next, with most of the air particles settled at the bottom layer. "Bottom layer," you remember, means the layer that lies against the surface of the earth, the troposphere. This layer is the most important part of the atmosphere. This is where you are sitting or standing at this very moment. It is a good place to begin our chart of the six hundred or so miles of atmosphere that extend above you.

TROPOSPHERE, the level next to the earth.

Height — about 8 miles

Temperature — gradually colder from the earth toward the top

Oxygen — more at the bottom, gradually less toward the top

Life — plants and animals, including man

Atmospheric conditions — clouds, sky color, sounds, weather; carries dust, pollen, spores, volcanic ash, and "star dust" from outer space

Exploration — by human beings on land, in

175

planes and balloons, and with radio and other scientific devices at all levels

STRATOSPHERE, the layer next to the troposphere.

Height — to about 40 miles above the earth

Temperature — steady cold, about seventy degrees below zero, all the way through

Oxygen — less and less with increase in altitude

Life — none

Atmospheric conditions — winds, cirrus clouds near bottom of level; nacreous clouds higher up

Exploration — by man in balloons and planes. By 1956 man had reached an altitude of nearly twenty-four miles in a rocket-powered jet plane. Scientific instruments carried by balloons and rockets have explored the entire stratosphere level and beyond.

MESOSPHERE AND THERMOSPHERE, the layers above the stratosphere.

Height — together extending 200 to 300 miles above the earth

Temperature — increases steadily beyond the stratosphere

Oxygen — very few particles, very far apart

Life — none

Atmospheric conditions — possibly vertical winds thirty to sixty miles up; noctilucent clouds

Exploration — by radio-equipped balloons and rockets. One rocket, Aerobee-Hi, reached a height of 163 miles. Another, Wac Corporal B, rose 250 miles into the air. Radar has also been used.

EXOSPHERE, the last layer of atmosphere.

Height — not known. (It may extend to an altitude of several thousand miles above the earth.)

Temperature — probably extremely high

Oxygen — practically none

Life — none

Atmospheric conditions — the last few, sparse bits of air spray out from the exosphere and into the infinity of space

Exploration — by radar, which has penetrated all layers of the atmosphere, many miles of space, and made contact with the moon

It is in the upper layers of atmosphere, at a height of 300 to 1500 miles, that scientists are planning to launch artificial satellites. If the plans work, the earth will have small, man-made moons in the upper atmosphere. The artificial satellites will carry scientific instruments to record some of the things about the earth's atmosphere that are not now known.

Space men, space rockets, space travel, artificial satellites — these are some of the signs of today's explorations. In many ways the atmosphere and outer space are man's new frontiers of discovery, adventure, and conquest.

20

STARS

How many stars can a person see on a clear night? How many stars can astronomers photograph through a telescope? How many stars are there, anyway?

Scientists tell us that there are never more than 3,000 stars that can be seen with the naked eye at any one time. But there are about 30,000,000,000 stars (yes, thirty *billion*) that can be seen and photographed through a telescope. And beyond the range of even the most powerful telescope ever made (the Big Schmidt in Mt. Palomar Observatory in California), there are doubtless many more billions of stars scattered out through limitless space.

Our sun is really a star. Other stars are probably much like the sun. Some of them are smaller, some larger, and all of them much, much farther away from the earth, so far away that it makes one's head spin to think of the great distances in space.

Perhaps some of the billions of other stars have solar systems revolving around them just as the earth and other planets travel around the sun. "Perhaps," say some scientists. But we may never know. We do know, however, that all of the stars are like our sun, and that there are billions and billions of them in the universe.

Go outside on a clear, moonless night. Try to find some spot where there are no city lights to interfere with your view of the sky. If you live in the country, go to the top of a hill. In the city, a good place for stargazing is the deck or roof of a tall building where there is nothing between you and the stars but the miles of atmosphere and the velvety black of outer space. Or, in city or town, lie on your back under the stars in your own back yard after the lights have been turned off in your house and in the other houses near you.

Use an ordinary flashlight as a star pointer. In your mind, divide the sky into sections and count the stars in each section. Every time you count a hundred stars, put a mark on a paper or drop a marble or stone into a can. When you have pointed out and counted, as well as you can, the stars in all of the sky you can see, add up the markers. How many hundred stars could you see clearly? Were there some stars that looked so close together that you could not count them? Did you notice that some stars looked larger and brighter than others? Did you notice any differences in color among the stars? Did some seem more yellow, some more red? Did you discover that stars make patterns in the sky?

As you counted stars, you may have discovered some of the star pictures or constellations. Constellations are groups of stars that seem to form pictures. These star groups were watched thousands of years ago by ancient stargazers who gave them names. Some of the ancient names are still used today — Cassiopeia (Queen's Chair),

180

Orion (Mighty Hunter), Canis Major (Big Dog), Taurus (Bull), Leo (Lion), and many others. There are nearly ninety constellations in all, but only certain ones appear in the part of the sky you can see at any one time.

To get acquainted with constellations, begin with three that are visible all year long. They are the Big Dipper, the Little Dipper, and Cassiopeia. To find them, look at the northern part of the sky. The Big Dipper is easy to find because it looks exactly like a big dipper. This constellation is sometimes called Ursa Major, or Great Bear. But, since it really looks more like a big dipper than a big bear, we usually call it that. When you have located the Big Dipper, look at the two stars at the side of the dipper, opposite the long handle. These two stars are called Pointers. If you draw an imaginary line beginning at the Pointer star at the bottom of the dipper, through the Pointer star on the Dipper's rim and extending straight out for a distance about five times as far as the distance between the two stars, you can locate a fairly bright star. This is the Pole Star or Polaris. The imaginary line away from the rim of the Dipper may extend in any direction in the sky, depending on the time of night and the season of the year. But, whether the line points away from the horizon, toward the horizon, or in between, the Pointers always point to the Pole Star.

The Pole Star seems to be the pole of the sky, the point around which the other stars move. Polaris always stays in the same place, always in the north, and about halfway between the horizon and the zenith, the spot in the

181

sky directly overhead. Whenever you face the Pole Star, you are facing north. You can see why the Pole Star was important to early sailors, before the time of the compass.

The Little Dipper is easy to find in the north sky. It is near the Big Dipper and looks something like it, only smaller. The Pole Star is in the very end of the handle of the Little Dipper.

After you have found both the Big Dipper and the Little Dipper, you can locate the third constellation, Cassiopeia. Imagine a line from the handle of the Big Dipper, through the Pole Star in the handle of the Little Dipper and out beyond it. This line will point to five stars spaced to form W or M. This is Cassiopeia, a small, bright constellation in the Milky Way.

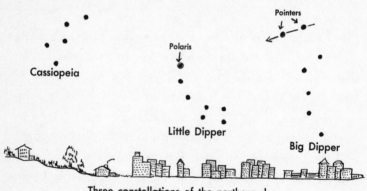

Three constellations of the northern sky

On clear nights at any time of the year you can see the Big Dipper, Little Dipper, and Cassiopeia. Locate them in the sky and watch them for several hours as they move around the Pole Star. The Pole Star, remember, stays in about the same place in the sky night after night while all the other stars revolve slowly around it. Once you have learned to find the Pole Star in the north sky, you can find different constellations moving around it. You will need to look at some star maps in library books, study the main constellations, one at a time, and then find them in the sky. Here are some to find after you are familiar with the two Dippers and Cassiopeia.

In the winter sky, look for Canis Major (Big Dog), Orion (Mighty Hunter), and Taurus (Bull). Of these three constellations, Orion is the easiest to find. Go outside on a clear winter night. Face south. There, near the middle of the sky, you can find Orion. You can recognize it by the three stars that form Orion's belt. Above the belt, at Orion's left shoulder, is a large, bright star named Betelgeuse. On one side of Orion is the constellation Canis Major. It includes the famous Dog Star, called Sirius, the brightest of all stars. On the other side of

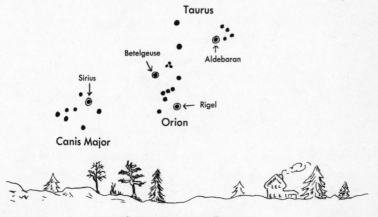

Three winter constellations

Orion is Taurus, the Bull, with its two long horns. This star group includes another bright star, Aldebaran, which shines with a red-orange color. There are many other bright constellations in the winter sky. As you learn to find your way among the stars, you will discover more of them.

In the spring and summer, look for Leo (Lion) and Hercules. Both of these constellations are found in the southern part of the sky in those seasons of the year. Hercules, a large constellation of many stars, is toward the east. Leo, with the bright star Regulus as one of its paws, is toward the west. Find out about other constellations that are visible in the southern sky during the summer. Some of them are Eagle, Scorpion, Harp, and Northern Cross. The Northern Cross is part of a larger and more beautiful constellation called the Swan.

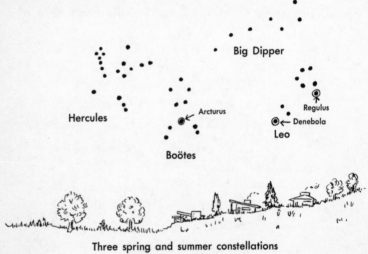

Three spring and summer constellations

You can have fun making and using a star box. Collect as many empty oatmeal boxes as you can find. Take off the cardboard lids carefully and save them for your next experiment. Turn the boxes upside down and draw dots for the stars in one of the constellations on the bottom of each box. Then, with a large nail, punch holes where you have marked the dots. Use the constellation pictures in this book or in a star book to guide you. Write the name of the constellation on each box.

Take your star boxes and your flashlight outside with you some night when you want to find the constellations in the sky. Hold the lighted flashlight inside the box. The holes you have punched will look like stars in a constellation. Look at them carefully and then search the sky until you find the real star pattern in the sky. Your star-box diagrams will help you identify the constellations.

You can also make and use a daylight "telescope." This is not a real telescope but something you can make to help you learn the different constellations. You will need one oatmeal box and as many extra box tops to fit it as you can find. In the bottom of the box, fit a cardboard tube eyepiece into a hole exactly the same size. If it does not fit tightly, fasten it with a strip of adhesive tape. On each of the box tops, punch out a different constellation, punching the holes from the inside to the outside.

To use your cardboard telescope, put one of the box tops onto the oatmeal box. Hold the box toward the light. Look through the eyepiece. Do you see the constellation?

Which constellation is it? Try the different box tops, one after another until you can recognize each one by name. As you collect more cardboard tops, make pictures of more constellations to study.

If you want your daylight telescope to look more like a real telescope, paint it black, and mount it on a frame so that you can move it up and down and around. In this way, you can always turn it toward the light and see the star holes shining at the end of the dark box.

It is fun to test yourself and your friends on recognizing the patterns of constellations in your star box or your daylight telescope. But the greatest adventure is always in finding the real constellations in the star-sprinkled skies at night.

As you search the sky for star groups, think of the prehistoric hunters, the early shepherds, the ancient sailors, and other stargazers of long ago who watched these same star pictures with wonder and awe. Some of the watchers made up stories about the constellations, stories we still like to hear today. If you are interested in the stories of the star groups, look them up in library books. Find out what the patterns look like in the sky, and the tales that have been told about them for hundreds and hundreds of years.

Draco (Dragon)
Cepheus (Husband of Casseopiea)
Boötes (Herdsman)
Lyra (Lyre)
Cygnus (Swan)
Gemini (Twins)

Try sleeping out in your yard some warm summer night. Before you fall asleep, or when you wake up during the night, and again very early in the morning, just look up into the sky and think about the billions of stars. They are yours all year long to study and to wonder at. You can see them and enjoy them even though they are millions and millions of miles away.

INDEX